T0149367

STILL
RHYMING

SUE A. MCLAUGHLIN

 iUniverse®

STILL RHYMING

iUniverse books may be ordered through booksellers or by contacting:

iUniverse
1663 Liberty Drive
Bloomington, IN 47403
www.iuniverse.com
1-800-Authors (1-800-288-4677)

Because of the dynamic nature of the Internet, any web addresses or links contained in this book may have changed since publication and may no longer be valid. The views expressed in this work are solely those of the author and do not necessarily reflect the views of the publisher, and the publisher hereby disclaims any responsibility for them.

Any people depicted in stock imagery provided by Thinkstock are models, and such images are being used for illustrative purposes only.
Certain stock imagery © Thinkstock.

ISBN: 978-1-5320-2043-8 (sc)
ISBN: 978-1-5320-2044-5 (e)

Library of Congress Control Number: 2017904680

Print information available on the last page.

iUniverse rev. date: 03/31/2017

DEDICATION

To anyone who chances to come upon
One of my poems, large or small,
Inspirational, humorous, poignant or pensive,
Or, perhaps you may want to read them all.
I pray that one of them touches your heart.

And to the One who inspired each and every one of them,
Whether sensible or silly, profound or off-the-wall,
May it always be said of me:
I heard and heeded my Master's call.

_____Sue A. McLaughlin

Contents

Section 3: Lilting Limericks

Section 4: Kissin' Cuzzins

Section 5: Lighthearted

Section 6: This 'n' That

Still Rhyming

My Penchant for Writing Poetry

Still Rhyming

Before the ink is dry on the last pages,
Before the last keystroke has been struck,
I am busily adding more rhymes to my repertoire,
Plus those old ones not making the first cut.

This compulsion for rhyming is compelling,
I seemingly operate in automatic,
I need another bit of doggerel as I need
The sunshine—and I'm frantic.

I write and write to no avail,
Except to keep my nimble fingers moving,
And my engorged brain is constantly
Spewing out so something I'll be proving.

I'm not at all sure what it is, exactly,
That sends my fingers flying o'er the keys;
But I'm grateful for the talent God gave me—
Sometimes it actually brings me to my knees.

I've said it often before, I write because I write;
And until I can't, I will continue
To bombard my friends and family
With my rhymes—that's what I do.

My Muse

My little fat fingers careen o'er the keys,
Journaling my thoughts, recording my dreams.
Noting my visions for posterity,
Planning my plans, scheming my schemes,
Composing, creating, authoring, writing
Down everything that comes into my mind,
Entering all the data that my Muse deems.

She's no respecter of time, the clock's nothing to her,
Gives no thought to situation, position or place,
Circumstances notwithstanding—she remains unaware
Of fatigue or of drama—she gives me no space
To renege on the pre-ordained, designated tasks,
Those goals that my life revolves around.
She's there, always there in my mind, in my face.

Some day when these dexterous digits have stilled,
And my mind is no longer able to wonder,
My Muse then must stop and go plague another,
Perhaps one more worthy than I to receive
Her assistance, her insight, a mind she must plunder;
An enthusiastic participant, recipient, receiver,
Eager and willing to have one's mind rent asunder!

Rhymer

Once a day, at least, I sit here
Writing rhymes on my computer, "Baby",
Scribbling verse on scraps of paper:
Something unforgettable, maybe!

The life of a poet is unrelenting,
Time after time I think this is the last;
But, then, another thought I must jot down
About my present, future or my past.

I read the works of other poets.
Some I really wish I'd been the one to write.
Some I truly wish I'd never even read!
Some I think I might actually recite.

Free verse does nothing for my psyche—
Yet, rarely, I, too have succumbed.
But even then I do believe that genre
Must "sing", so to the depths I've plumbed.

My favorite mode of expression always will be
The lines that spill across the page in rhyme.
For all that avant garde stuff and lower case "i's"
I really never want to waste my time.

A lot of people say that I'm old-fashioned,
But how many free-verse authors can you name?
While I can name a slew of rhyming poets,
And not just the one who made up "puddintame"!

I'm not saying that they aren't worth reading,
Nor am I implying I am better than they.
It's just that rhyming seems to be my M.O.,
I'll keep it that way—that's all I can say.

Perhaps I use my writing to escape reality—
Don't we all?
Maybe I'm procrastinating—
That's your call.

It also is a way of journaling—
Here I seldom come up against that wall
That often stops me from continuing
To give vent to feelings one and all.

Christmas Note

It's Christmas time again this year,
And time to write to those so dear.
Miles and means keep us apart,
Sometimes out of mind, but not of heart.
Time and tides and schedules demanding
May keep us all from corresponding.
But now I'm sending this little note
So I can say at least once I wrote.

No Telling

What do I write about today—
The aches and pains that beset me?
The twiddles and twinges and ouchies,
Or that pesky glitch in my memory?

I never thought I'd see this day
When listing maladies would be fun.
I have always avoided people like that
Who'd complain till the setting sun.

Now my anomalies head up the list
Of my daily topics of discussion.
Oh, not that I verbalize them all that much,
Except to show off my erudition.

I try very hard not to bring it up—
Discussing operations I detest intensely!
I'd rather be considered a positive one,
Not avoided for my negativity.

But here in the privacy of my own home
I can regale my old computer with woes;
It won't take affront or regard me askance
And never, ever, turn up its cute little nose.

So I'll speak of my glitches and globules and more
Of that which makes we quiver and wail,
And tell all my troubles and negative feelings
And everything in which I fail—or not!

Apology

I haven't touched you all day,
Nor yesterday, either, I fear.
What must you be thinking of me
When I usually keep you so near?
I didn't think you might miss me;
Worse yet, I didn't miss you;
You barely even crossed my mind—
What's this relationship coming to?

You who was once my life, my all;
You who sometimes was my everything,
Now shoved into the background
And made into a "sometime thing".
I can only throw myself on your mercy,
I apologize profusely for my slight.
You will always be my one true love,
And I hope that makes everything all right.
I love you, Baby. (my computer)

Doggerel…..Or Poetry?

Is it doggerel or poetry?
That's a question that I find
Is asked by many people
Who really ought to know.

But there's many a silly jingle
That still comes to my mind,
While the so-called classic poems
Not one line do I know.

So, write it as you feel it,
Even if it doesn't rhyme;
If it's doggerel or poetry
It's still not a waste of time.

If someone someday reads it
And remembers just one phrase,
Your reward will be undying,
And that's what really pays.

It's for you to tell the difference
As you read these pages,
As I rhyme my way through life
With verse from all my many stages.

A Need

No one seems to understand just why it's so important
That my book's accepted by a publisher.
Everyone wants their poems read by others,
We all think someone out there will really care.

The need to feel important to others,
To have their writings read by everyone,
And, yes, the need to sell that writing—
Recompense equals acceptance, to anyone.

I need to *be* important to my family.
If they say I already am, it doesn't show.
There's no feeling that I'm someone
They are proud to say they know.

Perhaps it's just for me I need it published.
A sense of accomplishment my flagging id requires.
This urge to write never seems to leave me,
This compulsion to see it in print is one of my desires.

If you also write and have not yet been published,
Only then can you actually understand.
No wonder publishers are thriving!
It's a big business, throughout the land.

Nobody is really helping with my dilemma;
I can't expect another to feel the same as I, and still,
Few can comprehend my feelings on this subject,
And maybe no one ever can or will.

Keeping On

I'll keep on writing poetry
Until the day I die,
Or maybe even longer—
In the "sweet bye and bye".
I've heard it said in Heaven
You get to do what you love the most,
But there will be no "bragging rights",
For there you cannot boast.
A shame, I think, for up there
I could do my very best.
I would finally accomplish
That which would make Him impressed.
I think I could hold my own there,
Allowing for changes in vernacular;
'Tho not a Poe nor a Shakespeare
I might still pen a poem spectacular!

Winging It

Tonight I'm simply winging it,
Free-wheeling, if you will,
Writing that which pops into my head,
Whether or not it fits the bill.

Rhymes about all sorts of things,
Pain and aging and sadness.
Lines of "what if?" and "if only"—
That road leads to madness!

For the most part I know why I'm writing
And where my mind and pen are wending;
Invariably my thoughts are optimistic
And usually have a happy ending.

Sometimes I simply feel like rambling;
Writing what I feel like writing.
No real reason or forethought,
Just whatever sounds inviting.

Most likely, it won't be important at all—
Often just trite and silly;
But if it comes to my mind, I know it's from Him.
I write with Him, not willy-nilly!

Compulsion

I can't seem to handle a pen or place a finger on the keys
Without itching to put my errant thoughts on paper.
Whether journaling or composing a story that makes one weak in the knees,
Or penning a poem or essay with which someone may find favor.
    It's all the same.
    It's the name of the game.

I'm addicted to computers and paper and pens;
It's a compulsion to give vent to my thoughts.
I pour out my dreams and imaginings and then
When trying not to, it's a battle hard-fought.
    I scribble, I doodle,
    It's all in my noodle.

I've written other poetry on writing,
Perhaps another one isn't something that I need.
I'll still continue as if some wrong needs righting;
I truly am obsessed, I am indeed.
    And writing I will do
    Until the moon turns blue.

I simply must get it down for posterity
Whether posterity ever reads it or not.
I'm not overly concerned with the clarity
Or if it's a writing that will someday be bought.
    Never mind the spelling,
      The muse is quite compelling.

If I keep writing poems I'll never finish my book!
But enough! It's time for completion.
Tucked up in my cozy computer nook
I will write with not much deletion.
    I'll stay up half the night
      To pen this just right.

I've maintained that God has given me the ability
To put my ramblings on paper for others to peruse;
But He hasn't yet told me if it's all futility
Or if this talent I may someday abuse.
    I guess I'll just pray,
      And keep on for another day.

Uplifting—

Enriching
Encouraging
Edifying

Talking with Jesus

Walking along on a sandy beach,
I felt His hand on my shoulder!
I was startled, to say the very least;
At first I believed it something bolder.

In an instant I knew the truth of it:
Jesus had come to converse with me!
I was elated, excited, if slightly appalled,
To think He had come to spend time with me.

I knew I hadn't been close of late,
My walk with Him left much to be desired.
Oh, I really still loved Him, of course,
But knew too much in the world was I mired.

I hadn't committed any major crime,
I hadn't ever slandered or lied,
My hands were clean and I felt pretty good
About myself—then why was I so petrified?

I knew deep within my heart of hearts
That I wasn't doing all He wanted me to do.
I wasn't spending time with Him, as He'd like,
Nor doing the things He required me to.

He didn't say all those things—
He simply smiled at me and said,
"Come back to me, My child,
I've missed you." So I obeyed.

Take My Hand

Take my hand, Jesus, lead me and comfort me.
Is it pride, or imagination or just plain lunacy
That leads be to believe that You will take my hand
And lift and carry me into that Promised Land?

I know I am not worthy that You should guide me day by day.
Of all women I am the most despised and yet I hear You say
You love me, and have done so even in my mother's womb,
And will ever continue to do so, yea, unto the very tomb.

Over the Threshold

It's an age old custom for brides and grooms
To carry the newlywed over the threshold
Into the first home that they will share.
It's supposed to bring good luck, or I've been told.

But I can't help but long for my beloved
To follow that custom to its inevitable destiny:
When Jesus carries me over the threshold of heaven
And welcomes His "bride" into eternity.

Scatter My Ashes

Scatter my ashes over the sea,
Cut the umbilical cord to Mother Earth,
I am ready to fly free.
Away from the mundane, the part we call life,
I'll fly to my Savior, as it should be;
And finally remain with Him eternally.

Scatter my ashes nearby, on a lake;
Tell no one—it's not legal—
Keep it a secret for your sake.
Do it for one who so loved the water—
I'm confident there is water in Heaven.
No momentous decisions do you need to make.

I'm grateful that no one will be gazing at me—
At a stiff, lifeless corpse in a box.
You know, who love me, how happy I'll be
To fly away to meet my Maker—
What sweet serendipity!
My Jesus is waiting to welcome me home
And guide me over that Heavenly sea.

Fling my ashes out over the waves,
Let my life and death show others
That it is Jesus who saves
And comforts and nurtures His children
From now to our graves;
E'en tho' "grave" is a misnomer,
For in this case, it's waves!

What a Beautiful World

What a beautiful world You've made, Lord:
That's not an original observation;
I know untold billions of people have said it
With varying degrees of elation.

The tranquility of the water,
The splendor of the sky,
The green stretches on for miles,
I want to take it with me when I die.

Oh, I know Your Heaven is more marvelous
But how can it ever surpass this lovely world?
It defies the imagination to even contemplate
A more magnificent landscape unfurled.

Lord, give me the eyes to comprehend
The grandeur and glory of Heaven;
Give me the heart to appreciate
That beauty seventy times seven.

What a beautiful world You've made, Lord,
And given to me for my appreciation;
I'll enjoy it till Heaven comes along,
Then I'll welcome *that* with utmost anticipation.

Faith

I asked the Lord, "Do I lack faith?
I ask in faith, believing,
With full confidence, that You will heal;
I pray and fast and praise,
Knowing that I am receiving;
Your answer comes, the miracle is real,
And I exult!
If I had enough faith all along,
Why am I so surprised You heal?
Why so happy You heard my appeal?"

And God answered with a story,
An analogy that He knew my finite mind
Would be able to comprehend.
He often speaks in parables to help us
Ordinary humans—He's so good and kind!
So wasted time in reasoning we would not spend.

"A man owes you a sum of money,
A check he soon to you will pay.
In short order you actually receive that money.
You know it belongs to you that day.
You never doubted you'd get it, you see;

But even upon receiving that paper piece
It is not truly yours—you can't exchange it
For goods or services or to give your heart ease
Until you take it to the bank and there
Receive the cash you were entitled to.
Knowing was not enough.

Even the confidence that it was coming to you
Does not make up for the elation
That now the money in your hand is what was due.
Now you not only have faith and believe—
You *know* that it is yours!

So praise My Name when miracles occur,
Even if some doubt crept in when praying.
I can and have done many miracles
Without a prayer or word worth saying!"

Better and Better

I'm getting better and better every day,
More healthy and happy in every way,
My body and spirit and soul are well,
My mind is wonderfully clear as a bell.

I don't want to simply slip out of this life,
To leave behind all the cares and strife,
But to boldly step into the New World with You,
Confident I've accomplished all You wanted me to.

I'm getting better and better each day,
Much better than yesterday, I'd say;
Not a problem will I consciously borrow,
And I'm not nearly as good as I will be tomorrow.

I want to be well, not for myself alone,
But for all my discrepancies I want to atone;
And I need Your good health to do and be
Everything that You meant for me.

I'm getting better and better I know,
And it's You I thank, as daily I grow
In the knowledge that You are caring for me
And giving me health, happiness and energy.

On Mothers' Day

God has a soft spot in His heart
For Mothers He has blessed.
He has an especial fondness
For those who've passed the test!

Be assured you are in His heart
And mind. And all our prayers
Are with you on this Mothers' Day,
For in Him you've had a part!

Christmas Card

A star was born that night so long ago,
And died that men may know that star.
He's still alive, and so
We'll be when Him we know.
Jesus is the reason for this and any season!

Church on the Square

There's a little church upon the Square,
With many kind and loving people there.
It wasn't always thus, you see—
Not long ago they saw the need to be
A congregation called by God,
To gather near this city quad,
Where many lives and hearts were broken,
And myriads of prayers unspoken.
God called them all to fill a need:
To preach against the vice and greed,
To minister to each hapless soul,
To help them all, that is their goal.
Everyone is welcome there
At the little Church upon the Square.

You Are Blessed of God

Dad, you are blessed of God.
You've sired and raised a child.
Though that daughter may be a terror
And that son be terribly wild.

You've taught them and loved them
And nurtured and led.
The way's not always been smooth,
Sometimes you've even bled.

But you know God forgives *your* foibles
And rewards *your* success.
So with those children He gave you
You can certainly do no less!

Enjoy the blessings of *your* Father
And know that you've done your best.
God honors His men that are fathers:
Yes, Dad, you are truly blessed!

Praying Trees

I so enjoy the view that I'm afforded,
The glorious trees I out my window spy,
Waving happily to the snowy clouds,
Their leafy arms uplifted to the sky,
As if in prayer to their Creator;
I ever smile at them and sigh.
I also offer up my eyes and arms in praise.

Personal Psalter

Reading through the Bible I keep Psalms for the last.
I like to read the Psalms on my computer
Where I can separate them, not dwell on the past.
A Psalter of praise and happiness, if you will.

Israel and David had their conflicts,
There were many, many times they fell,
But I prefer to concentrate on joyful praises
As if their woes and worries I could hope to dispel.

I love their stories—really, I do,
But often I just want to praise the Lord.
I want to read the verses that exalt Him,
I want to concentrate on the good news in the Word.

So, forgive me, Lord, for rearranging the Psalms
To read the way that I want them to be:
A paean of praise, exultation and love
To You, Your creation, Your consummate deity!

My Eulogy

I thought I'd sing a song for my memorial service:
"Going Home", perhaps, or "If You Could See Me Now";
But that was not to be.

Then I thought that my son or Pastor could do it,
As they would know how I feel, somehow.
But that would not be me.

So my memorial will be this poem,
To be read by anyone who cares to know
How I am feeling and what dying means to me.

Everyone that knows me knows
I love Jesus more than life.
So you know how happy I am to be finally free from strife.

I had a terrific childhood and a great family;
I have fabulous children and I know it.
I'm proud of each and every one of them—
Not one of them could blow it!

I devoted my life to my children,
Still, I made a multitude of mistakes;
They never had cause to be ashamed of me,
And if I didn't always do right, that's the breaks!

I tried and failed at many things,
Whether teaching or writing or sign.
I worked hard at everything I did—
Guess my best was poetry and graphic design.

I must have "retired" two or three times,
Only to begin again another career.
Trying to find what God wanted of me,
What He wanted me to do down here.

I loved my church and my church family,
And happiest when feeding the hungry.
In my small way I believe I helped
Many people that came to me.

I leave this old earth not sorrowful or sad,
But happy to be "graduating"!
My prayer today is that each one of you
Will join me in joyous celebrating!

There was certainly some sorrow in my time,
But I've been gifted with selective memory!
I remember only the occasions
When my life seemed to be carefree.

But, after all, I know this lovely life
Was but a fleeting moment in eternity.
I wasn't really quite "at home" in this body,
Always knowing there was more for me.

I made mistakes, I cried a thousand tears, perhaps,
But every time I knew to Whom to run.
He picked me up, dusted me off,
Set me on the right path until I was done.

I studied to be a teacher, and instead,
I was taught by life and God and circumstance;
I endeavored twice to be a dutiful wife,
But that didn't "work"—was it just happenstance?

If there is someone here who can't be glad,
Because they really don't know Jesus,
Now's the time to ask Him into your heart.
Be assured He always sees us.

Confess that you're a sinner, as we all were,
Before we decided to trust in the Lord.
Just tell Him you love Him and will follow Him,
And devote yourself to Him and His Word.

Now, see, wasn't that easy?
Now I will see you one day in Heaven.
We are both children of the Most High;
He forgives us seventy times seven!

God Made Me

God made the tiny mushroom
　And the mighty redwood tree
　　And me!
　　　Thank You, Lord!

Contented Soul

In every life I pray you encounter one
You truly know has a contented soul.
It's rare, but not impossible to know
When someone you meet has met His goal.

I know of one, a lady, who really was contented
To live in this world but not be caught up in it.
She served others as naturally as if born
To that special calling, not chafing even a little bit.

Serving with her husband for many fruitful years,
She carried on, when he was gone, for many more.
She seldom preached, or led a congregation,
Nor ever tried to put herself before.

Her ministry, mostly one-on-one, was well received
In this country, and definitely overseas.
Her warmth, her wit, her compassionate nature—
What you saw in her was, mostly, Jesus.

The contentment of the Lord was in her countenance,
Her demeanor reflected His joy and peace.
At 94 she is still praying for people and their needs,
And I doubt that this will ever cease.

I Knew the Time—or Not

I knew that I was going to die—
Oh, not the hour or the day,
Something inside I thought was God,
And I was ready to obey.

I felt no sadness at the thought,
Only an acceptance of destiny.
I began to think in terms of "last",
Last Christmas, last visit, last time I'd see.

A feeling very strong in me
Made me plan for my demise;
I thought much about Heaven
Trying each scenario on for size.

I felt I was facing the end of my life—
I wasn't ill or even unhappy;
Just resigned, perhaps even embracing death,
To all it will come, inevitably.

Another evidence of God's sense of humor—
That was over two years ago—
Or His way of saying, "I'll tell you when.
What makes you think you can say when you'll go?"

A Mother's Prayer

Jesus, I ask You to help me!
I know that You hear all my prayers.
Today my son really needs You,
And doesn't yet know how to ask.
But I know what You've done before in his life,
So I'm asking for him—and for me.
He's going out today and he's frightened;
Only You and he know the reason,
But the fear and the sorrow are real.
Still his mind and his heart, Lord,
Quiet his spirit to hear You,
Then hold his hand today, Lord.

I Asked the Lord

I asked the Lord for something that I wanted
And He said, "I gave you life!"

I asked Him for a gift to better serve Him,
And he answered "I have given you great gifts.
You need to discern them, then to use them."

I asked the Lord for a word in season,
That I might give it then to those in need.
He replied, "You have My Word—
Accept it; read it; live it; share it!"

Charge Your Battery

You gotta charge your battery!
A dead one's just no good!
It doesn't get you goin' anywhere.

At church on Sunday morning
You'll get a fresh jump-start
To keep your light a-burnin', if you care!

But did you ever figure
That your battery *should* be weaker
If you've been shinin' brightly everywhere?

But stop!
Get your batteries charged up!
Stop!
With the Word of God!
Stop!
Jump-start your
Mind and heart and worship,

With His prophecy and praise,
With prayer and with
Fellowship in His house.

What's Wrong?

If you don't feel the happiness in your church,
If you don't see the joy that's meant to be—
Don't look around you to see what's wrong,
Say instead, "What's wrong with me?"

Praying together side by side,
Working together with Jesus as our guide,
Striving ever to achieve that pride—
That pride that we are Christians!

If you don't feel commitment in your church,
To the Lord and to each other,
Search *your* heart to understand the cause
Instead of your sister or your brother.

Praying together side by side,
Working together with Jesus as our guide,
Striving ever to achieve that pride—
That pride that we are Christians!

Jeremiah

Long ago in Judah land
Jeremiah was a prophet of old.
Wonder if anyone ever called him Jerry,
Or would that have been much too bold?

A simple youth when God appointed him,
He knew it and tried to tell that to the Lord.
Who touched his mouth and reassured him
He would give Jeremiah the word.

He promised He would fill his mouth
With God's own words—to the nations.
Jeremiah would be God's own harbinger—
Warning Judah of all the altercations.

He never married or produced offspring;
He spent his life as just God's prophet.
He lived under good King Josiah's reign,
And five others—none saw fit

To take heed of the prophecies he made,
E'en tho' they were from the Lord's own mouth;
They simply couldn't fathom that He meant it—
They would one day understand it was the truth!

But try as he might to tell them, the people did rebel.
Despite incarceration and exile, he lived to a ripe old age.
He was released but stayed with his people who remained in the land.
Becoming even closer to God, this wise old sage.

A New Song

I need to sing a new song to You!
To thank You afresh for the things that You do.
I need to sing a new song to You!
To sing about the joy I feel
When following You!

Gift

Life is a gift, a glorious, unexpected, unearned gift
That I don't ever want to take for granted or underestimate;
And sometimes in the midst of this gigantic gift
Are myriads of vari-sized gifts I never could imagine
And never, ever could my finite mind anticipate.

Such a gift was that one rainy morning.
I was expecting a sunny day on this momentous occasion,
A wedding day that I'd looked forward to for quite some time;
But God ordained a very rainy morning—but a little later—
When the sun came out—the rain had packed the sand
So firmly that now I could walk upon it—much to my elation!

God give these two the gifts You've given me,
Of life and love and perpetual, everlasting anticipation
Of what you have in store for each of them and one another,
And the service that You've planned for them will cause them
To always be open to Your leading, with no hesitation.

Lord, thank You for Your plentiful, marvelous, unmerited gifts,
Bestowed upon a mostly undeserving world and nation.
I especially love the small surprises that You have in store
For us who love You—before we even think to ask it of You!
Oh, Lord, I know it's love that is Your motivation

The Reason

Is this not the time of the coming of Spring?
Is this not the time when a new world's in bloom?
Can you deny the Reason for the joy within your being?
Does your heart not expand to make room . . . .for Love?

Not in this Life Alone

I'm not in this life alone,
Tho' I have much for which to atone.
I've got a partner, a helpmeet, a friend,
Who'll stay by my side e'en past the end.

I know I am never without a comforter,
Without a confidante, a helper,
I cling to His hand as He helps me along;
I am happy, contented, filled with song.

I'm not by myself, existing on my own,
I am never in this life alone.
I will always have His calm assurance
To uphold me and provide endurance.

I may be perceived as being a solitaire,
But it's only an illusion, for He is there.
He gives me peace and joyfulness,
I know I need accept nothing less.

If I could convey one truth to you,
I pray that I actually could imbue
The reality that has become my own:
In this life you are never really alone.

Sympathy

Because we're children of the Lord,
I can empathize with you.
I can tell you that I've been where you are now.
No platitudes, nor a Scripture verse or two,
I'll simply remind you that you will cope, somehow.
Because I know to Whom you belong,
I know you will overcome, you will be strong.
God will most assuredly bless you and keep you
In this "valley experience".

Hot Miracle

I placed my hand upon the stove
To test if it was hot, you see—
　　It was!

God sometimes honors even stupidity.
Immediately I asked for healing—
　　He did.

Cold water and the prayer I prayed
Showed God's magnificent mercy—
　　To heal.

Nary a mark nor scar remained,
Just a hand in all its beauty!
　　Thank You, Lord!

To Dad

Daddy, Father, Papa, Pop,
Call him want you will,
But call upon him often
And say you love him still.

If you are a father,
Give thanks to God above
That He's seen fit to honor you
With a child born from your love.

And if you've lost your father
Know that you still have one:
The infinite Father in Heaven
You'll have till you are done—and beyond.

I Want to Be Closer

I want to be closer, closer, closer to You, Jesus
I want to be nearer, nearer, nearer to You, Lord.
I want to be right there beside You, precious Jesus,
I want to be there hanging on Your every word.

I want to be with You, with You, with You, gentle Jesus,
I want to be with You, with You, with You all the way.
I need to feel Your presence constantly, my Jesus
I need to feel You with me every single day.

I want to be closer, closer, closer to You, Jesus,
In everything I think and say and do.
I want to be nearer, nearer, nearer, every day, Lord,
And let my life be one big "I love You".

Simple Salvation

I thought I could go home, dress up and come back to be saved.
I was under the impression I had to clean up to be accepted.
Would that I had known it was His love that would clean me;
If I had only realized it was so much easier than I suspected.
Many hard days and nights, of wrongs and rights,
It was just not what I could have ever expected.
But when it finally came, that glorious salvation,
I would do anything in my power to protect it.
And nothing I can do or say, believe or perceive,
Can ever, ever, ever affect it!

Gift to You

The best gift I can give you
Isn't really from me.
The greatest gift is Jesus,
The best that can ever be.

He came to earth on Christmas Day
So you and everyone can say,
"Come live inside me, Jesus",
For that's the only way.

To be happy, Lord,
To have eternal life,
I need Your arms around me
To overcome pain and strife;

I know that You love me, Jesus,
And I know You always see us,
So we accept Your love today
For it really is the only way!

Believe

Time after time I have comforted you;
Over and over I have granted your desires.
Repeatedly I have healed your wounds,
Caressed your scars, put out your fires.
    Why do you not receive?

Continually do I show you My love;
Frequently do I say "yes" to your requests;
Again and again have I held you in My arms,
Often I have shown you My peace, My rest.
    Why do you not believe?

I can do this for you! I can give you My all!
I can and I want to give and give and give;
You know I am capable, you know I can do it;
You must know I can truly forget and forgive!
    Why not let go and to Me cleave?

What are you waiting for—a miracle from Me?
Do you need, like the Pharisees, a sign from the sky?
You frustrate Me, my beloved child—
I give you all that you need, I try and I try,
    But, for some reason, you don't fully believe.

What will it take to convince you I'm true?
Will it take you forever to acknowledge this all?
Can I rest now, in knowing you finally get it?
Can you, this minute, irrevocably hear My call?
    Do you believe?

Daily Prayer

Lord, I offer You this day
All I think and do and say;
May it to Your glory be,
And, incidentally, strengthen me.

Mortality

One should always have an innate sense
Of his own, personal, mortality.
Not to be thinking too much of his demise,
As to be always aware of his own frailty.

He needs to know his tremendous potential—
It's essential to cultivate some degree of empathy;
To realize exactly where he is headed—
To have a sense of his own mortality.

May we always be aware of who we are,
And Whose we are in our entirety.
To be sympathetic to those we encounter,
To deal with them throughout eternity.

I Can't Sing

I can't sing, but I can praise my Jesus' name!
I can't sing, but I can praise my Jesus' name!
I can tell you about the truth that's in the Word.
    And I *can* sing,
        Yes, I can sing—
            Oh, I can sing
                About the beauty of the Lord!

On Time

Never too little, too late, nor too early,
He's always on time, no matter how it seems.
If this doesn't feel like the truth in your life
It may be because of *your* expectations, *your* dreams.

The first thing we are taught to believe
Is "Thy will be done";
Why do we argue or chomp at the bit—
Are we really ready to argue with the One?

Reconcile yourselves to that great truth:
He's always perfect in His timing.
He is not a poor poet,
Imperfect in His rhyming!

Tapestry

I'm but a tiny thread on the underside of this weaving—
This beautiful, gigantic, complicated tapestry we call Life.
From here it just looks like a bunch of tangled knots,
Full of trouble, controversy, pain and debilitating strife.

But we know the Master Weaver and we know that one day soon
He will complete this tapestry, smoothing out the rough places;
My insignificant portion of this much larger piece
Will finally makes sense, with all its curves and spots and spaces.

So I'll not simply focus on this knotted, tangled woven work,
I'll concentrate on the right stitches and use the proper thread.
My workmanship will be perfect, my sewing even above par,
And most of all, I will only use the materials He's provided,

Trust

I pray for trust in You, my God—
This is not so much a poem as a prayer;
I am discouraged—I don't want to be, You know that.
My faith has not always been there.

My discouragement comes because I do not trust enough;
Why? You have always, always come through for me and mine.
I have no logical reason not to trust You,
You constantly have filled me with Your new wine.

I beg You, Lord, to help my unbelief!
Increase my flagging faith, abolish all my doubt.
Though situations may look dark and hopeless,
I have no rational cause to rant and shout.

I have full confidence in what You have in store,
I really do put all my faith in You—I must!
You have the only answers for me, my city and my world,
But please, Almighty God, help me to trust!

Andrew

Andrew was the quiet one. He didn't write a book,
He wasn't larger than life, he wouldn't make you look
At him and realize what a man of faith and conviction
He was, and between him and his brother there was no friction.
He was the first to acknowledge Jesus as Lord,
But he knew that Peter would follow.
And their love, you might say, became an addiction.
They followed Him all the days of their lives.
They were both martyred for it and left no kindred nor wives.
They brought many converts to Jesus, the Lord,
And were instrumental in spreading the Word.

Time to Be a Christian

I didn't have time to be a Christian,
I didn't have time to sit and pray.
Oh, there were times I talked to Jesus,
A word or two along the way.

I didn't know how to beg forgiveness,
Or what to beg forgiveness for.
I didn't ask Him to come into my life,
I didn't even crack the door.

But He came in anyway,
And He taught me how to pray.
He showed me how He loved me,
And I gave my life to Him.

Prayer of Relinquishment

Dear Friend, I am praying for your healing tonight.
For the absence of discomfort and beginning of peace.
With every ounce of my being I want you whole again,
And back where you belong, but with pain's surcease.
Whether from age or illness or whatever the cause
I pray your distress will find a release.

And then it occurred to me, perhaps it's your time.
I would never want to pray against God's will:
It may be that you're tired, or have completed the task
That He's required of you: your assignment fulfilled,
You've accomplished what He has told you to do.
So, rest in Him now, may your conscience be stilled.

Albeit, now, with a grieving heart I send
A prayer of relinquishment up to God's ear.
I surrender my will to the Father of all,
And hand over to Jesus a friend I hold dear.
But His will, not mine, and not even yours;
And if this isn't your time I'll definitely cheer.

So now, my dear Friend, I hope there's more time
To say all the things that we both want to say;
I know it's past time to do things together,
But perhaps there will be a time and a day
For pleasant memories and conversation.
We will surely be united in Heaven, one day.

Borrowed Time

One speaks of borrowed time as if it were a commodity
That we could buy or sell or barter or give to another.
Would that we really could borrow a bit of it once in a while.
We could perhaps do some good if that could happen—
A few more seconds when we are happiest
Could indubitably make each one of us smile.

A few more minutes or hours or days to bring someone to the Lord
Might mean a difference in their immortal souls,
And that would mean so much in all our lives;
It would benefit God's Kingdom, too,
To ascertain another saint be added there.
To that end is something to which everybody strives.

I know it's foolishness to even contemplate it,
But, in a way, we are, all of us, living on borrowed time.
We know not the minute or the day or hour
When God will "call in His markers" and "that's it"!
For at that time, borrowed, stolen or granted,
We will surely know His might and power!

We live for just such a time as this,
And speak so blithely of borrowing time,
When, instead, we might be better using it well.
Push on, stop dithering, and imagining such things.
We are allotted only a modicum of seconds
To work out our salvation. Choose Heaven or Hell.

That sounds so harsh, you are thinking,
But what other alternatives do we ultimately have?
You will agree, we all need to make that decision.
We may need to borrow a chunk of time to help us do it,
Or hopefully, have already come to the right conclusion.
If we're really going to borrow time, do it with precision.

I'm sure this notion of borrowing time is not one you haven't thought of,
For everybody does, at one point or another;
It's just a fleeting, foolish, idea that circulates through my mind;
And, all in all, it's rather fun to think of all the repercussions
That this "borrowing" thing can do to our imaginations,
And all the pleasant musings, fantasies and conjecturing we find.

Fresh Start

I write a lot about fresh starts
And the changes that enter one's life:
The happy, the great, the encouraging ones
And those that can cut like a knife.

I love fresh starts, as I've already stated:
Mondays and moving and mornings.
I love new beginnings and starting all over—
Even events that occur with no warnings.

But I've not yet told of the Fresh Start
That's the greatest, biggest, most important of all—
The day one starts fresh with Jesus,
That's the one thing you'll always recall.

That hour when you accept Him
Into your heart and mind and soul,
All that has gone before is forgiven
And in His Kingdom you now enroll.

A fresh start, a new beginning for you
They call it "the sweet bye and bye".
An inauguration of epic proportions,
The commencement of which we must comply.

No words can define the happiness we'll find,
At home at last with Jesus.
Sublime culmination of all of our dreams,
The moment when He sees us!

If the Foundation be Destroyed

If the foundation be destroyed,
What, then, can any do?
Swept off our feet, washed away,
What can there be, in lieu?

What we believed and trusted in,
Everything that we once knew,
Comes crashing down upon our heads;
To faith we say, adieu.

The lessons we had all been taught,
The beliefs we've held since birth,
Are now in dust beneath our feet,
Crumbled into the very earth.

Faith, Hope, Love, Joy, Charity,
There is now a shortage, nay, a dearth,
Nothing's good now, nothing's bad,
There is naught left of any worth.

If the foundation be destroyed,
We would be undone, forsooth!
We would never know of Jesus,
And never know the Truth.

There's a sermon in there somewhere,
But I'll let another preach it.
I pray you'll listen and take heed
While a better one than I doth teach it.

Almost Home

My goal is close to realization,
My journey's nearly completed.
The epitome of all my expectation
Is nigh—I'm almost Home!

The culmination of all my dreams,
All I have anticipated,
The fruition of my earthly schemes
Is close at hand—I'm almost Home.

There's little more that I could ever wish,
I'm happy that the end is close at hand;
From good and bad I can distinguish;
It's all good—I'm almost Home.

It's not a time of sadness,
Nor is it a time I would want to delay.
It is definitely a season of gladness—
Heaven's my destination and I'm almost Home!

Epitaph

I'll not have a headstone,
A marker for when I die;
But if you need that for closure,
Take this to remember me by.

SECTION 3

Lilting

Limericks

.....and some that are not!

Limericks

I am finding it fun to write limericks
About each friend and acquaintance
    Whose approval I seek:
    Each one is unique
And require very high maintenance.

Some are easier to write than others,
And if I had my druthers,
    I'd just write them all down
    With nary a frown,
'Cause they're all like sisters and brothers.

So some of the best ones don't expect to find,
And some of the worst come to mind;
    But most are the best,
    There's none I detest,
Because, as they say, even "like" is blind.

Virgil

There once was a man named Virg
Who was smart enough to merge
    With a lady named Jan
    Who knew a good man,
And to tie the knot they felt the urge.

But this isn't the end of the story.
This merger lasted, don't worry!
    For a great many years
    Through laughter and tears,
This wasn't just a mild flurry!

So now he's having a birthday,
And to make sure it's also a mirth day,
    I made up this limerick
    So he'd laugh himself sick
While I sing to him "Happy Birthday"!

Vicki

There once was a lady called Vicki
Who was most certainly never "icky"!
    A lady with class,
    Unusual in this morass,
But then, I don't want to sound "sticky".

Her façade is really quite beautiful,
Her temperament usually most wonderful.
    She is good and she's kind,
    She really has a great mind,
And also a daughter quite dutiful.

She has added a lot to my sojourn here,
And for most of the people far and near.
    She's "aces", by golly,
    She's sometimes a "polly"
And I count her a friend so dear.

Goodbye Vicki

I can't create the pretty cards I used to
That's just the way it is!
But I can still rhyme a little,
Tho' not like those in "the biz".

We all want to say "so long" to you,
But we'll never be able to say goodbye.
We expect you to visit often.
To say we won't miss you would be a lie.

Thanks for everything you've done,
And just for being you.
Hope you'll remember us, maybe?
So for now we'll simply say:
Hasta la vista, Baby!

Renaldo the Ugly Bug

One night I was searching for something on which to crunch,
But that bug in the cupboard looked like he wanted *me* to munch.
    I'm not sure if roaches bite people, or not,
    But I felt like I was in quite a spot.
I didn't want to wait to meet more of his bunch.

It was the ugliest, most disgusting, revolting, big insect
For which I never had, never will, have any respect!
    They are gross and vulgar and actually obscene.
    God knows on them I have never been keen.
Maybe irrational, but on me they had an adverse effect.

I determined once and for all to conquer my fears,
To go on the defensive and annihilate the little dears!
    Armed with a spray and a heavy duty fly swatter,
    I reopened the cupboard and watched them all scatter;
To my amazement, none of them deigned to appear.

From the corner of my eye I saw a tiny black shadow,
And there by the stove were three in a row.
    I went down on all fours,
    Opened all the cupboard doors,
And attacked the pernicious creatures that I loathed and deplored.

Lo, and behold, it must be my day!
They scattered before me as if to say,
    "Okay, you got me, now go on your way,
    We'll go somewhere else—wherever you say!"
When the last one had vanished, I called it a day!

Early the next day, a brand-spanking new morn,
I felt such relief, like I'd been actually reborn!
    Till I opened the cupboard to face once again
    The ugliest, most horrible sight within my ken:
Renaldo was back. I felt as though I was looking at porn.

But this time I was ready, despite my surprise,
I plunked him with my newspaper—that's how a bug dies!
    I felt I had done such a good deed,
    Killing my nemesis, and not even bleed.
And, on top of that, protecting my delicious pies!

Of course, as you know, that wasn't nearly the end
Of my ugly bug problem or the things I intend
    To do to keep down the roach population.
    Maybe an armistice with this bug nation.
No, I need to destroy it, lest I go 'round the bend!

So, with sprays and bombs and, finally, the exterminator,
My enemy was finally vanquished—I was "The Annihilator"!
    My friends all called me to help them out,
    They thought I knew what it was all about!
I was the hero, Renaldo, the perpetrator.

Farewell, Renaldo, rest in peace—hopefully, piec-es!

Gout

There was a young lady with gout
Who didn't know what it was all about;
    Her footsie was swollen,
    Her joy it was stolen,
The pain she could sure do without!

She got around in a chair, in or out,
But, I must confess, with a pout;
    No longer a go-getter,
    She wanted to get better,
And then she'd be happier, no doubt.

Tim

I know a man whose name is Tim.
He'd never leave you out on a limb.
    He's funny and furry,
    Never in a big hurry,
And never hurt you on a whim.

His birthday happens to be on 5/2,
And this year, would you believe, he's 52?
    How cool is that?
    So put that in your hat,
And that should never make him blue.

Lonny: Happy 60th Birthday

I'm fond of writing limericks, so here goes with one
To commemorate my first-born son.
    I could write something mushy and gooshy,
    But I never was one to be pushy,
So I'll write what I write about Lon.

We've always been close to each other
And not just as a son to his mother;
    Perhaps it's just a bit spooky,
    We are both a trifle kookie,
But we seem to understand one another.

I remember a little tow-headed wonder,
Who was known to pull a blunder;
    He was ornery and charming,
    Usually quite disarming,
Always climbing in or over or under.

Recently he's had some trouble keeping healthy,
But he's kind and wise—but not so much wealthy.
    A man of whom his mother could be proud,
    And even at times a little bit wowed!
But she keeps that information rather stealthy.

Hence this limerick, the longest in history.
So here's to the guy who's somewhat of a mystery.
    As we celebrate a whopping sixty years,
    Through much joy and success, laughter and tears,
So I'll stop now—I don't know what rhymes with mystery.

For Jesse and Emily

I wanted to make you something special
'Cause you both are special to me.
I used to make afghans for weddings
Back when my fingers flew so free.
Now it takes a little longer to do
What I once did so handily!
I don't know about the colors you'd choose
If you could somehow inform me,
So I'll give you ALL of God's colors,
Or a reasonable facsimile!

Jesse

There once was a young man named Jesse;
We all know that he is the best. He
 Is handsome and kind,
 And it always comes to mind
How good he was in his ministry.

His musical ability is legendary,
His vocal talents incendiary!
 His entertainment was fun
 It made the Devil quite undone.
His puppets made one feel merry.

Then he met and married Emily;
Their love was plain for all to see.
 They knew how to have fun,
 And put the blues on the run;
Complementary in their ministry.

Emily

Emily was a lady of excellence,
She had truth and beauty and good common sense.
    She seemed just made for Jess:
    They sure ain't no mess!
And she is so very far above dense.

I don't know too much of her background,
But even in college I sure liked her sound,
    When Jess explained how
    They met, he said, "Wow!"
And told everyone he'd like to have her around.

So now they both labor for the Lord,
And are busy happily spreading God's Word.
    They sure make a difference,
    And even by inference,
Are adept at wielding that two-edged sword!

Jimmie

There once was a guy called Jimmie,
He was anything but an enemy;
    Tall, dark and handsome,
    Sweet, funny and winsome,
Ever a good friend to me.

He was really quite a man,
As a husband or driving a van;
    A driver extraordinary,
    Other motorists better be wary,
Accidents just aren't in his plan.

Thirty-some years with wife, Gloria,
He'd never deliberately worry ya'
    He is so helpful, everyone knows,
    He makes friends wherever he goes.
They don't live in the Waldorf-Astoria!

Retirement Rhyme

Did you think that I leave without a poem?
Just some rhyming lines to tell you how I feel?
    I'll assail your ears with jingles
    As indigestible as Pringles,
So I won't expose the feelings that are real.

It's eleven years and seventy-three days now
Since first I came into these hallowed halls.
    It hasn't all been charming,
    At times it was alarming,
Looking back at all my errors and "prat-falls".

I may work many other places
Before that final retirement year,
    But those I chance to meet
    Must go some to beat
All the lovely people I've met here.

I have to say that I am glad to leave here,
But there's one thing I must note before I go:
    It's really sad to say goodbye,
    And before I start to cry,
I'll state, "I'll miss you more than I can say."

Retirement Isn't an Ending

R eady to face a new challenge
E very brand-new day;
T hankful for where God's brought you,
I n each and every way.
R etirement isn't an ending,
E njoyment of life is the key;
M ake the most of this new beginning,
E nter your new destiny.
N ow is yours for the taking—
T o live, to laugh, to be happy!

Matt

There once was a young man named Matt,
Who tho't he was "all that"!
    When it came to girls
    He chose only the pearls,
And in sports he was ever up to bat.

His IQ was quite astronomical,
His demeanor at times quite comical,
    He was handsome and true.
    And could laugh right on cue.
His living was most economical.

Matt was always true to his friends,
And that quality sure reaped dividends.
    Work ethic, tremendous,
    Disposition, stupendous,
He seldom was forced to make amends.

Matt was also a Godly man,
One you could count on, never ban:
    A guy you could trust,
    Love him, you must!
So I did and I do and I can!

Two Peas in a Pod

Mark & Carol, two peas in a pod,
Alike in their love for each other and God.
    Through the ups and the downs,
    There were smiles, there were frowns.
Through it all, He gave them a smile and a nod.

Many trials they withstood, made many mistakes,
But at the end of it all, they were merely "out-takes";
    Loved by their family,
    They'll go down in posterity
As two who had more happiness than heartaches.

Rhoda

I have to tell you all of my friend, Rhoda.
She's really built, you know, like a brick pagoda.
    Her attributes are many,
    Her faults—she hasn't any,
At least not ones you'd ever dare to note.

She sometimes can be volatile, it's true,
But to become her friend you wouldn't rue.
    She's loyal to a fault,
    And sweet as chocolate malt,
But not syrupy-sweet, don't misconstrue.

She'll tell it like it is, I have no doubt,
But sometimes has a tendency to pout,
    But, all in all, true blue,
    A friend who sticks like glue.
And friendship's really what it's all about.

Christmas Throw

Here we go, a Christmas throw
To keep you warm and cozy.
Not much, I know, as great gifts go
But it will make you nice and rosy.
You may use it now or at Holiday time
To throw across your couch;
Think of me who thought of you
With every stitch, I vouch.

Richie

There once was a guy we'll call Richie,
So mean my trigger finger was itchy.
    He married a woman keen on baking
    And made her laugh till her sides were shaking.
But in the end she turned bitchy.

Richie was a man who made you laugh
And never did anything by half.
    Lori was his lady love,
    They fit together hand in glove.
And he looked at her with eyes of a calf.

Maggie

I once knew a lady named Maggie,
Whose features were never saggy!
    She was happy and spritely,
    A real "Holly Go-Lightly",
And never wore clothes that were baggy.

She was all the time helping her neighbors,
And forever doing them favors,
    She became a fast friend,
    A friend to the end,
Sweet as all Baskin's 31 flavors!

Louie

There's a man I know, named Louie, who is
             really quite a mensch.
A gentle man, a nice man, truly a gentleman,
             that's a cinch.
    He never tried to tarry with me,
    Even offered to marry with me,
But we never thought it wise for us to hitch.

When we first met I called him "Trouble".
But he's pure gold, not hay and stubble.
    And the more you get to know him,
    You'll know he really isn't dim,
So I wouldn't ever want to burst your bubble.

A friendship with him would never be moronic,
Our feelings for each other were quite platonic.
    A friend who sticketh closer than a brother,
    A true friend, really like no other.
He's as fun and effervescent as a tonic.

Chuck

There once was a man named Charles,
His friends all called him Chuck;
    He was personable and loquacious
    With an apartment that was spacious,
And décor that certainly doesn't suck.

He has traveled widely everywhere,
And met many people who still care;
    He's done many interesting things to talk about,
    And known many people with a lot of clout,
And done things that perhaps some wouldn't dare.

Chuck's a kind and gentle man, generous to a fault.
If you begin to be negative he will soon call a halt.
    Everybody's friend is he,
    But nobody's fool, you see,
Friendly, open and garrulous is his default.

Father

F is for the fantastic Dad God gave me,
A for the awesome things he's done for me,
T is for the troubles, and there've been a few,
H for hurts and heartaches he's seen me through,
E's for eternal treasures he's helped me store within my heart. I'm
R eally blessed to have the father God gave me at the start.

Vacation Rhyme

Is there a question you want answered,
Or a problem you want solved,
A price list you want finished yesterday?
Feel free to start your search within my files,
But you can see that might get quite involved,
Take heart, there is an even better way.
If you exercise some patience
You can outwait my vacation—
I'll be back on June's 11th day.

I'm Dreaming of a Green Christmas

I'm dreaming of a green Christmas,
Just like the ones I used to know,
    Where the treetops glisten,
    And children listen,
To carols everywhere they go.

I'm dreaming of a green Christmas,
Palms swaying o'er the manger scene;
    May the Lord bless each girl and boy,
    And bring everyone health and joy,
And may all your Christmases be green.

Little Black Bug

Once there was a little black bug that hid in cracks and crevices
To come out at night to plague me and to become my nemesis!
    I've told you before of my aversion to all crawling things,
        And flyers and slitherers and creepers and those with wings!
It's even worse if you detest the *thought* of their services!

They tend to startle and always surprise you,
No matter that you think you know what to do.
    They're no respecter of any class or race
        Age or ability—or disability may be the case!
The night, the dark places is their milieu.

Exterminators are the only answer to this dastardly pickle!
I don't pretend to defend them—I'd not be that fickle.
    I hate and detest them—that's not overstatement!
        If they all would keel over I'd not erect a monument;
I'll not cry when they're erased—not one particle!

Salute to My Nurses

I once knew a nurse named Yuri,
He was great taking care of you and me;
    His sidekick is Erin,
    She's not "Lee & Perrin",
But as spicy and helpful as he.

They taught me a lot of what I needed,
Tho' their help I somewhat impeded,
    I'll remember them always,
    To the end of my days,
Tho' that might not be too many, that's conceded.

Michael

How do I love you? Let me count the ways…
Oops! That's already been done
And by a much more erudite poet than I;
But I can write about Michael—my other son.

I love you most because you love my daughter
And brought back into her life romance and fun.
I love your ways—what I know of them,
Your faith, your values, how you treat everyone.

I appreciate your intellect—my daughter wouldn't
Date no dummy! The fact that you're cute doesn't hurt.
I know, looks aren't everything, but yours are pleasing,
I am ever quick to assert!

Your solicitude to her mom and kids
Are just icing on the cake.
But that all goes to show you
Michael certainly ain't no rake!

So I want to give you some accolades here,
And tell of my love for a special guy.
This is not very likely to change,
Just increase as time goes by.

Son-in-Love

This may not be included in "High on Life"
But, perhaps, here in "Still Rhyming",
But I'm just now finishing it
And it may not be the timing.

You are more than just a son-in-law to me,
And more than "just another son";
When God made you He threw away the mold—
You aren't "just another one".

You took me into your heart and home
And included me in your family.
You didn't really have to, you know—
Living with me isn't easy.

But you did and you do, and not just 'cause your wife
Wouldn't give you much peace if you didn't.
You're a thoroughly sweet and Godly man,
And not to love you I simply couldn't.

This is the first day of our lives
When I, too, am a part of your "quiver".
You certainly didn't need another one:
But your love flows outward like a river.

Yes, you are a son to me,
But you are also so much more!
Mentor, Pastor, pal and friend,
And one I can say that I adore!

Only One "Poppy"

There's lots of different Pops and Papas,
Dads and Daddies, Paps and Father;
A rose by any other name—said Shakespeare.
I go back in my mind to my own
And I've seen quite a few that were really no bother.

I loved my Daddy and even my Pappy but this one's unique.
A man like no other, husband, son, friend or brother.
What's to comment upon with a man such as this one?
To His children, step-children, grands, and greats
He is one in a million, unlike any other.

There are many men, perhaps, that you could mention
As being special to you, and I might agree.
But this one is distinctive, exceptional, exclusive.
Everyone who has met him will say the same:
There is only one Poppy, his love is the key.

My Favoritest Thing

I must award an accolade to my buddy!
He's one of my very best, favoritest things!
He's so very warm and toasty,
    He's nice and comfy-cozy,
    I might even say he's roasty,
I extol him for the comfort that he brings!

He is absolutely indispensable in the dead of winter.
He's become my best, best buddy, there's none sweeter,
    Something I needn't tend,
    It will not break or bend,
    It's my buddy, pal and friend,
You know, of course, I speak of my trusty heater.

To Kiki

Your sleek lines
Your shiny paint job
Your chrome and your mirrors—
Not just a big blob!

Your power and speed
Upon acceleration
Excites my libido—
Such exhilaration!

Your color so lovely,
Whether green or red,
You're not one of the pack,
You're always ahead.

Behind the wheel
I have nothing to hide.
I've a feeling of joy
And a comfortable ride.

I am King of the Road,
A feeling so free!
We are quite a pair,
My car and me!

Farewell, Kiki

I loved you not too wisely, but so well!
I wanted you so badly, everyone could tell.
    I nearly put my life on hold
      To keep you as I should;
Little did I know then
It was just more than I could.

Your gleaming exterior was mesmerizing,
Your bright red color was tantalizing;
    It wasn't a case of puppy love;
      I truly thought we were meant to be.
I rationalized to keep you,
But I really wasn't thinking rationally.

Kiki, you gave me such joy in my life.
Never once have you brought me strife.
    I would never willingly part with you,
      But one must know when it's the end,
When a chapter in life has closed,
Even when it means parting with a friend.

Judy

There once was a lady named Judy,
She dealt in all kinds of "booty",
    From crafting to creating jewelry,
    And all other kinds of Tom-foolery,
She just deemed it all part of her duty.

She would go wherever sent—
For entertaining, she just had that bent.
    Talented, charming and bright,
    She worked tirelessly day and night.
Judy made friends wherever she went.

Russ

'Twas the day before Christmas and all through the van
The passengers were smiling, down to a man;
The little old driver, so lively and quick—
I knew in a moment, it must be St. Nick. (a.k.a. Russ)
He jumped onto the bus with a leap and a bound,
Taking us and our packages without making a sound.
He helped everybody as slick as a whistle,
He made it seem as light as the down of a thistle.
Quickly and quietly he went on with his work,
When he was finished he turned with a jerk;
And laying a finger beside his nose,
He plopped into the front seat, in driver's pose.
Then gunning the motor, he drove out of sight,
Saying, "Merry Christmas to all and to all, good night!"

My Neighbor

I must tell you of my good neighbor,
A hero without cloak and saber.
    Once he did, in fact, require,
    The Fireman's aid with a kitchen fire,
But mostly being good is no labor.

He's good at cajoling all the girls,
Even those no longer sporting curls.
    He does what he can
    To be a real ladies' man.
If they ask, he might even offer to shoot squirrels.

My Babies

I had quite a few kids, you see,
One of whom was Jamie Lee;
 He was delightful and cute,
 And really quite astute,
For the boy that was number three.

There was also Lonny Dee and Marky Doo;
They were number one and number two:
 Funny and charming,
 Both quite disarming,
My mainstays in all that I do.

My girls were Jenny Sue and Becky Jo,
My lifelines in my old age, you know.
 Smart and pretty,
 And oh, so witty,
It was such a delight to watch them grow.

And then there was Tommy
The "baby" for this Mommy;
 You'd never know it to see him now,
 He's grown to quite a man—and how!
And as beneficial as edamame!

Of course, there's Baby Keith in Heaven,
That rounds out the number to seven.
 Him we didn't get a chance to know
 And never even watched him grow,
I know he would have been a man among men!

Kissin' Cuzzins

Correspondence Between a Country and City Cousin

KISSIN' CUZZINS

Feb.22, 2005

Dear Cuzzin Carrie,

Got your Christmas newsletter
Quite some time ago.
I'm glad y'all are doin' so well, but
Your family never seems to grow.
I know your kids are perfect
And you wanted me to know.

So now I take my pen in hand
To finally answer your letter
And tell you how it is with us,
For now we're so much better.
'Cause I know I owe you a note
And I sure ain't no debtor.

My second son, Bobby Joe,
Announced the other day
That contrary to opinion
He's really proud of bein'' gay.
But he's got another partner,
Much to our dismay.

Matilda has been gone awhile:
Ran away from home a few months back.
She says that she still loves us
But she just felt a lack.
Even all the boyfriends she had
Couldn't keep her on track.

I guess you haven't heard yet
That my Mindy had a baby.
The cutest little baby girl,
She is quite a little lady.
Her daddy ain't nowhere around
So Mindy named her Sadie.

My Hiram Lee is workin' now—
Got a job down in the stock yard.
His hours are long and pay is suret
And he's workin' mighty hard.
But it's really good for him
To work off all that lard.

Little Cindy—'member her?
She's finally gettin' wed!
Thought she'd never land a man
This side of bein' dead.
Frankie finally asked to marry her
When she wouldn't git in his bed.

My old man, Sam, is back again.
He was gone for quite a spell.
I didn't know just when he'd be out
And it seemed no one would tell.
But now he's home with all of us,
Unless he lands hisself back in jail.

Good thing there weren't no more kids
For I couldn't take the hassle.
My hair turns even grayer
Every time them twins rassle.
I know you think I've got too many
And I admit this is quite a passel.

So enjoy both them perfect kids.
I've been dyin' to tell you about mine,
And thought this a good time to do it.
You know I love each and every chile
And I sure ain't complainin' none.
I just wrote this all to make you smile.

I'm too tired to write some more—
I'll write about my twins next time.
There's so much more I want to tell you.
The other day one ate a dime!
They sure do keep a body busy!
And to think I really wanted nine!

Love, your Cuzzin Maddy

Mar. 30, 2005

Dear Cuzzin Carrie:

You remember my twins, Maude and Claude.
One's a boy and one's a girl,
Alike as two peas in a pod.
There out there now a-rasslin'
On our new, just-put-down sod.
When I looked out my window
One of them was throwin' a clod.
They won't be but nine years old
Next July twenty-nine,
And times they're much more trouble
Than tryin' to make this here rhyme.
It's just one scrape to another, why
Last month Claude up and ate a dime!

But one thing I'm used to is problems,
And I knew just what to do.
I made him drink from the slop bucket
And, boy, howdy, it came through!
Guess he won't be doin' that again,
And Maude learned her lesson, too.

If one twin don't think of somethin'
Then the other one sure will.
I'm grateful we're not at the old farm
Where my daddy had his still.
I'm feared we'd all be blowed up by now!
Them twins are sure a pill.

Guess you never had no trouble
With your two perfect children;
I'm glad for your good luck, Carrie,
Hope you'll be happy always
And never have no problems
Until they're both grown men.

I'll write more later,

Love, Maddy

May 5, 2005

Backatcha, Maddy:

I must try to write this nice,
'Cause Montgomery doesn't like it
When I revert to my hillbilly days
And talk like I never left it.

But sometimes it's so hard
To say what I want to say,
Remembering to speak good English
And use my words right, as they say.

I was glad to get your letters,
You have such an exciting life.
I get pretty bored here in the city
Being the perfect Mom and Wife.

In spite of what you tell me
I know your kids are doing great.
Please tell them "howdy" for me,
Glad Cindy finally has a mate.

My boys are doing dandy.
Monty's in college, come the Fall.
Larry really wants to go, too.
But he's not old enough, at all.

They both are making good grades
And dating nice girls, too.
They go to church on Sundays
But I don't know with who.

I miss the good old days sometimes,
We were really quite a pair!
Madeline and Caroline—
We never had a care.

Then you went and met Sam
And I married shortly after.
Montgomery Aloysius Pinckney, III—
That name gave us some laughter!

Now I am rich and you are poor
And you have lots of children.
But upon our relationship, dear Maddy,
I do reflect quite often.

So write again, my cuzzin,
And tell me all the scoop.
I'll be waitin' for a letter
And I'll read it on my stoop.

Your Cuzzin Carrie

July 7, 2005

Dear Cuzzin Carrie:

Are Monty and Larry serious
About the girls you say there datin'?
Are they a-spoonin' on your stoop
Or just dancin' and ice-skatin'?

Hiram Lee is datin' now,
Or so you might be callin' it;
He visits Sally only once in a while,
He's so tired he just stays for a bit.

Looks like he'll never pop the question,
So if Sally wants to marry him
She'll probly have to do the askin'—
That boy is really sort of dim.

Matilda Mae just called last night—
You know, she's the one what run away.
She says she's a waitress at Al's
And workin' really hard all day.

So she won't be comin' home real soon,
'Til she saves up some money.
Course I told her if she wants to come,
"I'll send it to you, honey."

Guess she wants to be on her own—
She was always independent.
And also a right stubborn little thing,
And for herself she's always fended.

I'll let you know if she comes to town.
Maybe you and the boys can visit me;
But I guess if you come you'll be alone,
'Cause your family doesn't like my family.

That's okay, you know, 'cause I feel the same.
Just don't cotton to the city.
So I won't be visitin' you, either,
And maybe that's a pity.

Got to go now…..love, Maddy

Sept. 4, 2005

Backatcha:

Maddy, I think you've pegged it.
Our lives just don't fit together.
You don't like it here, I don't like it there,
And I really do hate your weather.

I like to be near the ocean,
Those hills and woods ain't for me.
You all living the country life
Is far more than I can see.

So I guess you're right about visiting
But maybe some cold day.
You just never can tell in this life,
So I'd hardly like to say.

Say, are you going to leave me hanging?
You said Billy Joe was gay.

Is he living with his partner?
What did you and Sam say?

I don't know if I could handle it
If Monty or Larry told me that,
But, again, I'd hate to say.
I don't have an answer down pat.

I guess I'd just go on living
Like we always used to do,
Cause you still got to love them,
And that's just what I would do.

Your loving Cuzzin Carrie

Oct. 13, 2005

Dear Cuzzin Carrie

Yep! You sure hit the nail on the head!
That's exactly what we done.
And that friend of his, named Peter,
Is just like another son.

Since they're both out of high school
They now live nearer town.
They have a little shanty
And are plowin' up some ground.

Say they both want to be farmers
And I don't see no strife;
So I guess that's what they'll do then,
Be farmers all their life.

Sometimes the twins go help them—
Don't know how much help they are!

But it keeps them out of trouble,
And they ain't a-goin' far.

They haven't done much foolishness
In quite a little while;
Could be that they are growin' up,
But at that I have to smile.

They surely are the ornery ones.
They're really both a menace.
Don't have a darn thing on
That comics boy named Dennis!

Got to get their supper on,

Love, Maddy

Dec. 15, 2005

Dear Maddy:

I like hearing about them twins of yours,
They must surely be quite the pair.
I never went through much of that,
My boys just wouldn't dare.

I guess they did their share of pranks,
But never told me or Montgomery.
He never stood for any nonsense,
But I knew they weren't as good as they could be!

Monty, Jr's girl's really something!
Got her head chock full of knowledge;
But I doubt they're talking marriage yet
'Cause he's determined to get through college.

My Larry likes to play the field,
But now he's dating a real sweet girl;
She's just the same age as him,
And her name is Dorothy Pearl.

Montgomery's still making pokes of money
And, I admit, I love to spend it.
But sometimes I get a little bored
With nothing to do but tend it.

I just bought a new-fangled wash machine
They call it state-of-the-art.
Sure wish that you could see it.
I had trouble getting it to start.

One day soon I'll get a drying machine,
And then won't I be ritzy!
But then I'll have even less to do
Except sitting around looking glitzy!

Mostly I am happy with my life,
But some day I may visit you
To see all them children you got and
Just for something different to do!

A little on the lonesome side…..Love, Carrie

Mar. 14, 2006

Dear Cuzzin Carrie:

Boy, that must be some fancy machine!
I know it must be some humdinger!
Does it have that little door on the top
Or does it have a great big old wringer?

What in the world is a dryin' machine?
Is it one of them-there called a dryer?
I seen a picture on the TV.
Sam just raised my clothesline higher.

I know I sure could use one
With washin' all baby Sadie's clothes.
Good thing we don't wash diapers no more
Or she wouldnt be smellin' like a rose!

She sure is growin' like a weed,
She's really shootin' up!
Can't believe my eyes some days—
She's growin' faster than the pup.

Sure is a pretty little thing;
I'm real glad now Mindy had her.
So we still don't know her papa,
That really doesn't matter.

Guess what the Good Book says is true:
He makes something good happen
Even out of something not so good—
Guess He likes to catch us nappin'!

Sadie's 20 months old now,
And quite a little singer!
All of us are crazy about her:
Got us all wrapped around her finger.

A neighbor come and took her pitcher,
So I'm sendin' a copy to you;
She said she just had to have one
And before she left she had near 22!

Someday you'll have a grandkid
And know how fun it can be
To dress them and to play with them;
Course it's still a lot of work for me.

More clothes to wash…...love Cuzzin Maddy.

June 6, 2006

Dear Maddy:

Maddy, you will never guess,
Not in a million years,
What I am going to ask you
Will give us all some fears!
And what I got to tell you
May bring y'all to tears.

Are we really second cousins—
I got to ask how close are we—
Maybe cousins once or twice removed?
'Cause it may be important
To the whole darned family!
Montgomery's in a tizzy
Wondering what to do.
I confess I'm not much better,
Thinking this might all come true,
But praying it will all work out—
I just don't know what to do!

Guess I'd better tell you quick
Before you have a heart attack.
Remember mentioning Mattie Mae
In a letter a while back?
I had almost forgot about it
And that surely is a fact.

Well, it seems my Monty
Went to a diner with his pals;
There was quite a few of them,
About 7 guys and gals.
And there—maybe you guessed it—
He met Mattie Mae at Al's!

He says he's really fallen hard
And he's broken his girlfriend's heart.
She thought she had him tied up tight
'Til Cupid threw his dart
And hit both Mattie and Monty.
Now they can't seem to stay apart!

Mattie Mae wants to marry Monty—
Maybe she's already told you.
Monty can't keep his mind on college
But he says he'll stay if we want him to.
Montgomery's fussed about the cousin thing,
So you'll have to tell us what to do.

We all really love your Mattie
And we can tell they love each other,
But whether we can let them wed
Is what we must discuss with one another,
Before they go and do something stupid
And that's sure not something anyone would druther!

Write quick!........Caroline

June 20, 2006

Dear Cousin Carrie:

Well, you and your Montgomery
Kin set your minds at rest.
We're really not that close a kinfolk
But even should I be pressed
To figure out just how removed
As cousins, there's just no test.

My daughters in hog-heaven!
I finally talked to Mattie Mae.
She's floatin' somewhere on Cloud 9
And can't think of anything to say;
Except to talk about your Monty.

She asked me just what you did—
She was scared they couldn't marry.
Now that she knows they kin do it
They neither one want to tarry.

So tell me all your thoughts on this.

We need to get together…..Maddy

June 30

Dear Cuzzin Carrie:

Who'd ever have thought it?
Our kids is getting hitched!
They won't wait much longer,
You should see the fit she pitched
When I said maybe Christmas;
They both ran outside the house,
I thought that I was ditched!

So how about we plan September—
It's so nice that time of year.
The leaves will sure be pretty,
It will be real nice here.
We got so much room and all,
Your family will be welcome, dear.

Hurry up and answer......Maddy

July 1, 2006

Dear Maddy....or should I say future in-law?

It's something I would have never dreamed!
We couldn't have guessed this would happen,
Even if we both had schemed.
Watching these two together tells me
That they are both well-teamed.

Don't you and Sam worry none,
Montgomery wants to do the paying
We'll have the wedding at your place,
I think that goes without me saying.
'Cause you've the bigger family,
And you'll soon be finished haying.

You've got lots of land out there—
We can plan an outdoor affair.
So pray for lots of sunshine
To shine on the happy pair.
We want to do it all for them
So y'all won't have a care.

Maddy, when we said one day we'd visit
Who'd ever thought "one day"
Would be an occasion such as this,
Our children's wedding day?
We'll all have the time of our lives
Eating and celebrating, wouldn't you say?

So we'll be coming early,
Me and Dorothy Pearl and Larry,
Though Montgomery will have to work
And can't come till the day they marry.
But I'll be there to help with the planning
And believe me, I won't tarry!

Monty and Mattie will be coming this week;
Monty needs to meet all the family,
But nothing's going to hold him back
From still wanting to marry Mattie.
Our friendship will be even closer,
Now we're double-related, you and me!

Love, Your Cousin Caroline.

Sept. 25, 2006

Dear Cuzzin Carrie:

After all the excitement of seein' you all,
Boy, howdy! It feels a lot different now!
After the hullabaloo of the weddin' and stuff,
I just feel this big let-down, somehow.

Haven't heard hide nor hair from those kids;
Them honeymooners sure must be havin' a time
Not to at least once call their folks;
If I knew where they were I'd send them a dime!

Must be even lonesomer for you,
With only one kid left and him off to college.
But it sure makes us all proud
That your boys have so much knowledge.

We're all just startin' to settle down here
After all that fun it now seems like a wake.
We did have Bobby Joe and Peter over for dinner.
Peter even went and baked us a cake.

That's all for now, I need to get busy.
If you hear from Mattie May and Monty
Please be sure and let me know.
I miss them both, don't you?
But now I've really got to go.

Love, your Cuzzin Maddy

Lighthearted

Amusing
Whimsical
Satirical

Pesky Conscience

You can't always do what you want to do,
Whispers that little voice inside my head.
Does that mean I can't go skinny-dipping
When I should work—or even go to bed?

You need to set a good example
For all those folks around.
Does that mean I have to eat my veggies
Instead of consuming chocolate by the pound?

That sounds like a much better option
Than eating potatoes and meat.
I've never been so fond of veggies,
If I could choose something sweet.

Does it mean that I can't sit relaxing
In my rocker, reading a good book?
Or must I go to the kitchen instead
And begin to learn to cook?

Do I have to clean and scrub and dust
When I'd so much rather go to the beach?
Must I whip up pork and "chittlins"
When I'd rather just eat a peach?

Oh, it's just not any fun having a conscience
That's always telling me what to do!
I'm grown-up now and past the stage
When I have to always be listening to you!

So, get behind me, Conscience
And cut me a little slack.
If you continue with *that* dialogue
I never *will* come back!

Holes in My Walls

It always made me happy to poke holes in my walls!
Some of my early memories were of hanging pictures everywhere.
My Mom let me "decorate" the wall above my bed,
And every month I did that, consistently, I swear.
My early creative endeavors were flamboyant!
I bedecked the space with color, panache and flair,

Some places in which I lived just didn't allow it,
Government housing comes to mind—they were very strict.
I somewhat curtailed my decorating habits then,
But later I did it anyway, and thought they had been tricked—
Because when I moved I patched the holes and painted,
Tho' drab, off-white colors I, of course, picked.

I couldn't have lived in so many different places
If I hadn't put my mark upon the dreary, dingy halls.
I've always had this craving for color,
Grays and blacks and drabness isn't my style at all.
I admit it's somewhat an obsession to me;
I have this compulsion to poke holes in my wall!

Deck the Company Halls

Deck the Company halls with boughs of holly,
    Fa-la-la-la-la-la-la-la-la!
Dress we now like Pam and Dolly.
    Fa-la-la-la-la-la-la-la-la!

Everyone is gaily singing,
    Fa-la-la-la-la-la-la-la-la!
In the lunch room bells are ringing.
    Fa-la-la-la-la-la-la-la-la!

We all work like little elves,
    Fa-la-la-la-la-la-la-la-la!
Taking pride among ourselves.
    Fa-la-la-la-la-la-la-la-la!

Tho' we're in a festive mood now,
    Fa-la-la-la-la-la-la-la-la!
We accomplish our jobs, somehow.
    Fa-la-la-la-la-la-la-la-la!

So we say—and we're sincere,
    Fa-la-la-la-la-la-la-la-la!
Merry Christmas, Happy New Year!
    Fa-la-la-la-la-la-la-la-la!

What's In a Name?

I was named, officially, Sue, not Susannah as I wanted,
Which was my maternal grandmother's name.
Everyone thinks I've shortened it from Susan;
If that were so, 'twould be no one to blame.

What's really in a name, anyway?
When you're little lots of names they call you:
Cute, endearing names that show their love;
Or when they are irritated, they exclaim, "Sue"!

My daddy had a nick-name for me—
I was called "Sammy" for the longest time.
My initials were the origin of that, you see,
Even married my initials stayed the same.

"Susie", "Susie Q", "Sioux City Sue", "A Boy named Sue";
Then "Mommy", "Aunt Susie", "Grandma", "Grammy",
Until one set of grandkids called me "Mimi"—
For me I guess that was the "double whammy"!

Now, it seems, even at church they call me "Mimi":
But it didn't stop there, don't you know!
What's in a name, you ask? That may depend;
It's degenerated to "Meamster" and "The Meme";
I just can't tell if all this will ever end!

Under Stress

Our funny little "stress balls" are all shredded,
The FAX machines have never seen such traffic;
The phones are ringing and the lines are humming
With questions and with facts most geographic.

Everyone's preparing for this gigantic project
And my department is unusually frantic.
A line's been drawn across the sands of time—
The deadline's set for info both visual and semantic.

What are we doing? Why do we look this way?
Why does this seem like such an insurmountable task?
We've taken on the responsibility of input, layout and printing
For the '96 CIA* Directory—I thought you'd never ask!

*Correctional Institutes of America

Christmas Wish

'Tis a bit past Hanukkah
And all through the Tower,
All the inmates are stirring
To create a Christmas bower.

Everyone's hurrying and scurrying,
Some railing and ranting,
They've got their little heads together
Frantically pushing and panting—

Trying to make it all come to fruition.
We're all expecting a huge success,
A fabulous festivity
And not a big mess.

It will be a wonderful Christmas party—
Folks are busy as elves to make it so.
They're grinning and humming old Christmas songs,
Feeling so "Christmassy" tho' there's no snow!

The joy of the season permeates the room;
We're all working together with those who are near
To make it a joyous Merry Christmas
And a fantastic New Year!

Mom's Vegetable Soup

'Twas the week *after* Christmas
And all through the house
We were all sick of turkey
Yes, even the mouse!

When all of a sudden
My wishes came true!
A big bowl of vegetable soup
From out of the blue!

Guess it took a long time
To cook up such a treat,
But it sure tasted good,
All those veggies and meat!

On a cold winter day
I couldn't ask for more
Than a hot, spicy soup
To open each pore!

So Mom's vegetable soup
Still holds a fond place
In my Christmas memories.
Let us say grace!

Ode against the Philippines

Heat, mildew, humidity and rust,
Everything damp or gritty with dust,
Things that should open are stuck like glue,
Those that should close you'll never push to.
Houses as hot as the hinges of Hell,
Or as cold and damp as the bottom of a well.
Locks on the doors and lights on all night—
Your best bet is a dog that will bite!
If you're hit or cheated, turn the other cheek,
No matter how mad you get, pretend to be meek,
Or suffer the penalties of the brave and the bold—
At the very least, you'll be put on "Admin Hold".
Lock up your kids, your pets, husband (or wife),
Money and cigarettes guard with your life.
Crooks and con artists, to mention the best—
If one doesn't get you, beware of the rest.
Murderers, thieves, and a sprinkling of rapists,
All masquerading as such devout Papists!
These are some of the joys of this Philippine Island
That I can't seem to want to ever make my land.

Indecision

I have a problem, can't make up my mind,
To get dressed or remain in my housecoat?
That's, at times, a gigantic decision,
On a par with buying a house or a boat!

I can't decide whether to work today
Or dress and go out on the town.
It's six of one, half a dozen of another;
Sometimes I am up, sometimes down.

Perhaps I should go out shopping today,
There are a few things that I need.
But to make such a momentous choice
I might need someone to intercede.

Is this a sign of depression, you think,
Or my scattery brain on a strike?
It sometimes just seems to be too much
To pick what I hate and what I most like.

When I just can't really select *anything*,
When it's all too much for my little head,
I choose to pull the covers up to my neck
And curl up in my welcoming bed!

'Twas the day before Christmas

'Twas the day before Christmas and all through the store,
Employees were bustling and banging each door.
Each little old worker, so lively and quick,
With no thought of shirking, let alone being sick.

Through their heads danced visions of the day after this,
And how to best steal that mistletoe kiss.
On high, in the executive suite,
Our little old Santa's just leaving his seat.

Our illustrious leader, called "Abe", by name,
And our own Christmas Carol—you know—Gloria, the same.
And bounding behind them, came Bob, the chief elf;
I smiled when I saw them, in spite of myself.

The tip of a cigarette was clenched in his teeth,
And the smoke it encircled his head like a wreath.
As they came down the stairs, grinning ear to ear,
We all were aware we had nothing to fear.

At the very stroke of twelve on the clock,
Business would cease, and we'd all start to rock!
And I heard them exclaim, when the day was done
Happy Hanukkah and Merry Christmas to everyone!

Being Grownup Sucks!

I am long past the age of innocence,
Eons away from what I used to portray,
No longer can I claim "I didn't know",
Or any more pretend naiveté.

I every day must claim adulthood,
There's no way around it, I really am stuck.
Childhood is a very long time past,
But still I cry, "Being grownup sucks!"

I so wish I was a youngun once more.
I detest being among the muckety-mucks.
No matter what anyone says,
Being grownup sucks!

How I'd love to curl up on my Mother's lap,
Stick my thumb in my mouth and cuddle.
But that's not to be, I'm grown-up, don't you see,
And life is a terrible muddle.

If I could only insist on a do-over,
I know I'd be great and have a million bucks;
But I can't and I don't and I didn't,
And being grownup sucks!

Galloping Grumpies

I have a case of the galloping grumpies;
I'm miserable and have no desire to be
Sweet and nice, nor do I want to be pleasant;
I want to be mean and nasty and behave irritably!

I'm sick and I just want everyone to know it.
These walloping galumkies aren't fun, you know.
I got to get to feeling so much better
Before I can even write about it, so,

I'll just have to suffer through it—
"Montezuma's Revenge's" only here for a day.
So I will simply groan and sleep it away
Until those galloping grumpies gallop away!

Legend in My Own Mind

I was a world-renowned writer,
Writing away, at the top of my form.
Oh, that was just little old me,
Dreaming it all, tucked up in my dorm.

I was a 5-star general,
One of the few in the Women's Air Force,
Blonde and svelte and leading my troops,
Imposing and also popular, of course.

I was a famous graphic designer
The darling of the advertising world;
I could do no wrong, I was A#1:
They touted all my ideas as pure gold.

I was a gourmet cook with discriminating palate;
No critic in the land would disagree.
My dinner parties were a legend—
Simply everyone wanted to be invited to see.

Speaking before even heads of state,
I was a recognized yet humble preacher;
I knew what I knew and all knew it, too,
The most discerning wanted me as teacher.

I was a Mom, par excellence
Mother of the year material;
At discipline, I was extraordinary,
Until my kid spilled his cereal!

Of course, one of my well-known jobs
Was that of a true trophy wife.
The envy of my husband's acquaintances,
I led a fabulously glamorous life!

Then there was my career as a singer.
I was celebrated throughout the country,
Recognized for my truly dulcet tones,
Clawing my way up with impunity.

An actress was I, and a good one, at that.
Theatres all competed to book me.
I used every wile I could to advance
Before my great talent forsook me.

There were my days as a transient—
I adored being a beach bum!
Enjoying to the fullest the sun and the sand
And the free spirit that I had become!

At one time, a distinguished professor
Of art and English and literature.
I even became tenured—
I was the very picture of hauteur.

There was even a season when I was a nun.
Now I ask, can you picture that?
Whatever I am or wanted to be
That's as ridiculous as trying to be a gnat!

I was a notorious Madame
Make of that what you will!
While I am inventing personas,
Tho't that one might fit the bill!

Yes, I was prominent, legendary, great,
Famed and eminent, infamous.
In my own mind I was world renowned,
Celebrated and illustrious.

Guess everyone has some dreams in him.
The trick is in which one you'll finally find
The one that best fits you, or you fit it—
We're all legends in our own mind.

Universal Panacea

You're down, you're out, you're feeling blue,
The world's just not treating you as you wanted it to;
Your hair doesn't look right—what can you do?
    Go eat ice cream!

That guy—or gal—had the gall to dump you,
Through no fault of your own—why, you could just sue!
They've taken your heart and just ripped it in two.
    Go eat ice cream!

That test you took today—and this is nothing new—
Was just formulated wrong—not what you were used to;
No wonder you failed, nothing else you could do.
    Go eat ice cream.

Talk about the Universal Panacea—it's very true:
Whatever your problems, whatever you rue,
In the center of a Mall, in the midst of a zoo:
    If you go and get ice cream,
      It will all seem brand new.

On Aging—Again!

One sometimes ages gracefully,
With hardly a ripple upon the surface;
But a life full of care and conflict and sorrow
Shows the results of untiring service.

One seldom ages quickly, all at once,
Changes simply do not occur overnight;
The gradual deterioration of skin and flesh
Is evidenced only when you look just right.

My face is like an old road map
That's been many times folded and read;
Feet and legs are blotchy and puffy,
Less like 80 and more like a hundred.

I'm sagging and bagging through this life
Wending my way to the grave.
For face lifts and tummy tucks
I'm really not that brave.

I shouldn't put this little ditty
In any one of my poetry books.
Who really wants to read about
A lady who's losing her looks?

But my poems are like my journal,
So I think perhaps I will
Add it onto one of my volumes,
My autobiography to fulfill.

Eyes that once were sharp and clear
Now faded and rheumy and teary.
It's no wonder some days I succumb to ennui.
I now admit, I'm just plain weary.

It's just too late for some things,
Like exercise and wrinkle creams,
That firm the face and the body—
That's really just a pipe dream.

My feet are mottled and scarred,
And sometimes a trifle swollen.
It's as if the appendage I once was so proud of
A mean little leprechaun's stolen.

Legs and back, once so strong,
Arms that could hold, lift and carry,
Are now limp as a noodle,
No longer able to thrust and parry

I've "talked" about so many things
This is just one more.
A phase in my life to show
What an oldster has in store.

It's time to admit what I didn't want to—
I just ain't what I used to be.
So I'll be honest and enter this
Here in my poet's diary.

Cursivity

I am proud of that certificate of perfect penmanship
Received in early years, pertaining to my hand-writing,
According to the Peterson cursive method of expression.
And that is why I rant here and am strenuously plighting;
I am in opposition to those mighty moguls who have agreed to end
That graceful form—that's against whom I am fighting!
The demise of penmanship as we know it, could be disastrous,
And definitely, at the very least, will be very disquieting.
How will we write our signatures if we're never taught?
Printing may be very clear, but not so very inviting.
Lines and circles may be easier to put on paper,
But I don't find them graceful or extremely exciting;
I'm happy I can still write in a flowing, cursive manner
And hope this bit of doggerel some may find indicting.

Exercise in Futility

Night after night I play Solitaire on my computer,
Striving to beat the odds and increase my wins.
As if anyone in the world will ever see my statistics,
As if anyone knows when it ends or begins.
    It's an exercise in futility.

Day after day I get up in the morning,
I dress myself and perform my daily ablutions,
As if there was someone watching to be sure that I did it;
As if to all the world's problems my habits were the solutions.
    Another exercise in futility.

They say the definition of madness is doing the same
Thing over and over, expecting a different ending;
Tilting at windmills, trying to make a big difference,
I'm still watching the world in all its upending.
    Watching it all in its futility.

But never expecting to be or do anything significant,
Never trying anything because no one cares,
Is to never find happiness within my own existence;
It's never being that courageous one who dares
    To experience that exercise in futility.

My Brain is Full

Cease the madness! Stop the persistent bombardment,
The continual barrage of thoughts, pictures and dreams;
My brain is full! I cry, cease and desist!
After all these years I retain everything, it seems!
Ideas, quotations, phrases, facts and fictions,
Photos and fragments and glimpses and gleams.

When my eyes are open or whether they're closed
Through my mind they are whirling at a fantastic speed.
Lists I am making, trips I am taking, my body is aching,
But still it continues, that gigantic kaleidoscope I feed
With all my musings, meanderings, memories—
And they're not all always real, I have to concede.

My imagination is active, and that's as it should be,
My intellect's really a force of its own:
Didactic, moralistic, romantic, futuristic;
I see the past and the present and e'en the unknown.
It's like some gigantic motion picture screen,
But when I awaken, I find it's all flown.

I just can't stop the thinking, the plans, the designs,
Embracing my remembrances, forecasting the future,
I am ever projecting, organizing, arranging
Schedules and schemes, I constantly nurture.
For my life, my future, my present and past
I am really the penultimate researcher.

Imagine a college student—what he has already learned
And all he has lived, and watched and experienced!
Then double that panorama alive in his brain,
And factor in all he has thought and sensed,
Witnessed and daydreamed and put down on paper,
For which he feels he has amply been recompensed.

Cease this outpouring, my brain is so full!
I must stop this onslaught, it's disturbing my sleep!
Yes, I want to remember, I enjoy some of the dreams,
But too much of a good thing on my head it does heap!
If I am being assaulted—that's what I call it—
Quickly and soon out of bed I must leap!

I am glad for the memories and all the slideshows
That play out through my mind at a frantic pace,
But the timing's not right, it's just not the time,
And it's definitely not the appropriate place!
When I lie down at night, courting sweet repose,
Could we just put a hold on that feverish race?

Id Rules

Good thing you're cute, and have a disarming smile,
Or I would have left you after just a little while.
Oh, wait, that's just what I finally did!
I needed to do that for the sake of my id.

This 'n' That

An Eclectic Potpourri

Suddenly Summer

We've waited and waited, with bated breath, as it were,
Dreaming and planning for what is to come.
We've endured the ravages of "Old Man Winter"
And, actually, some of us have come undone!
We wondered if we'd ever make it through till Summer
And the joys and promises of Summer fun.

We dream of all the swimming pools we'll visit,
We plan for all those great excursions we'll take;
We just know that life as we know it will be sweeter—
We can even taste all the "Summer" of which we'll partake!
Watermelon, corn on the cob, hot dogs roasting on the grill,
Veggies fresh from the garden and strawberry short cake!

We're all looking forward so to Summer
That we can really hardly wait!
School is out, and life just more laid-back.
For the fireworks let's make a date—
What a magnificent display there will be
On a fine Summer night—you can relate!

Then, suddenly it's Summer!
All our wishes have come true.
The plans we made came to fruition.
The balmy weather's here, hot, too,
But not worthy of complaining—
We'll endure the heat to finally renew!

Summer is a precious time for one and all;
Summer is a sweetheart and a lover all in one;
The lovely mornings, sweet and fresh and clean,
The velvety nights of romance or of fun.
Somehow it's just more pleasant when it's not cold,
One feels so much happier basking in the sun.

It seems that we all eagerly await the Summer,
A change, a new beginning, the "sun's footprinter";
But all too soon we see it waning;
It's rushing as quickly as a long distance sprinter
Toward the other seasons, toward the cold—
And suddenly, again, it's Winter!

Thanks for the Cards

The cards you sent were lovely,
The sentiments inside were warm,
But the signatures within
Were the most appreciated.

I truly loved to get each one and know
That you remembered me.
Knowing you took the time
Made me totally elated.

I don't really need a card
To know how much you love me;
The special bond we share
Will never be outdated.

If I'd saved ALL the cards and letters
Sent to me throughout the years,
There'd be a couple of rooms
In which they would be crated.

So if you don't see your note
Just know that I love you
And they were all
So much appreciated!

Dolphin

I wanted to buy you a Dolphin—
The biggest and best in the world!
As a token of my affection,
And the fun we had at Sea World.

But my wants wouldn't equal my wallet,
And where would you put such a token,
If perchance I had purchased a porpoise,
And forever my budget had broken?

So, please accept this remembrance
Of the thought that was in my head:
To bring joy to you this Christmas.
I'm sending a picture instead.

Impressions from the Hospital

Fear, trepidation, anxiety,
Love, peace, confidence, trust,
Pain, itching, frustration and more;
Overpowering it all, faith is a must.

These are merely impressions of the observer,
What must it be like for the patient?
Not really understanding fully,
The only course open, to be simply obedient.

Lights and wires, beeping machines,
Computers, monitors, beds up and down,
A few days of laughing,
Soon replaced by a frown.

Nurses and doctors, so friendly and kind,
All the staff so accommodating,
Even at the very worst moments,
So gentle and calm and placating.

The feel of Mama's gentle hands,
Watching her sweet and smiling face—
As long as Mom's here
It's not such a bad place.

Praise God that the young patient
Doesn't realize the ramifications;
She has no basis of reference
Just feels results and elations.

A hospital is a world unto itself,
Distinct, different, completely unique;
The people, the patients, the ambience,
More impressions than I can possible critique.

And Think of You

When evening shadows slowly fall,
    And night comes on;
When the rosy sun peeps o'er the hill,
    And comes the dawn;
In darkest night so bleak and cold,
    When all goes wrong;
In brightest day so fresh and new,
    When life's a song:
    I stop,
    I pause,
    I meditate,
    And think of You.

When the gay lark sings no more
    And skies are gray;
When the flowers bow their heads
    And coldly lay;
When the sun shall cease to shine,
    Then cold the earth;
When all is gone and there exists death, not birth:
    I'll smile,
    Unafraid,
    Secure,
    And think of You.

My Day

The sky is blue, the grass is green,
The sun is shining bright,
For just today I'll be a Queen
From morning until night.

Everything will go my way,
And all day long I'll sing.
I shall be master of this day
And rule it like a King.

Today's a very special day,
There's something magic in it;
As if my life were pantomime
And I'll just today begin it.

I wouldn't want to trade this day
For a world of silver and gold.
This special day is my Birthday,
And I am ten years old.

The Wheel

Come, let us board that big blue bus on the corner,
I have something important I would like you to hear.
Please, sit with me in that seat directly over the wheel.
Let's listen to what it has to say.

It rolls along over city streets and boulevards,
It races over freeways and picturesque country lanes.
We'll listen as it whispers of the people all around us;
It will tell us of their stories, backgrounds and dreams.

We'll listen, too, as it sings of the wonderful places
It has been and the marvelous things it has seen.
We may even learn of its problems and desires
And perhaps learn to understand and appreciate it.

Then, when you have listened for a while
You will begin to realize something
Of the truly wonderful story a wheel has to tell—
If we listen.

A Mom's Mom

I thought about my Mom tonight
On the eve of another Mothers' Day.
I remembered fondly her voluptuous laugh
And the marvelous things she'd do or say.

I'm thinking mostly how she'd love you, my daughter,
And all those Godly traits that in you've been implanted.
She invented all those "Momly" things
That we, as Mothers, take for granted.

She knows in her omniscient way
The trials that you've lived through
That brought you to this point in time—
We recognize 'twas God's great coup!

But, mostly, I thought how proud she'd be
Of the Mom that you've become.
I know she's smiling through her tears
(She's the one we got that trait from.)

It's All About Me

Whatever the various circumstances,
Wherever I go, whomever I see,
In crisis, contemplation or joy,
It's really all about me.

I sincerely try to help other people,
I think, for the most part, I do.
I believe my heart is in the right place
But my mind sometimes hasn't a clue.

When it all comes down to the basics,
Except for the fortunate few,
We are all self-centered an selfish,
Myself, most of all, it is true.

God, what are You trying to show me,
Besides that it's all about me?
I know there's a marvelous lesson here
'Cause I don't think this is how it should be.

There's no doubt it is human nature,
We say, with some reservation,
But should I really be living for me—
It's not bad, it's just self-preservation.

Who will look after me if not I?
I know You desire I take care of me
But not to the point of obsession—
Does it mean I need therapy?

Where am I going with all this, you may ask?
Believe me, I'm wondering, too.
Is the answer just to "let go and let God"?
Tell me, what is Your view.

This poem is really going nowhere;
I am finished with thinking so deeply.
Someday I may revisit this question—
Is my life really all about me?

Monday Morning Mania

Weekends are pseudo-silent,
Everything a few degrees off-center,
Semi-somnolent, a little laid back,
Then, Monday morning mania enters.

It seems as though the staff swells,
The "regular" doctors are "at it again";
People seem happier, more refreshed
Than they were before the week end.

They're anticipating better things to come,
Of busy-ness and noise there's no lack.
They are all about business as usual,
Performing that which only they have the knack.

Monday morning mania is a good thing—
A brand-new start to a brand-new week.
This day could conceivably change everything,
Perhaps giving answers to that which we seek.

I Like Me

I like me—I really do!
I didn't always, that's so true.
There were numerous conflicts here and there,
That sometimes caused me not to care
About myself, and others, too.
Now that's been finally resolved.

My Vision

You showed me a body of water—
I felt I knew the people there,
But not the time or place.
Such an excitement You gave me,
And joy in fulfilling your promise!
Then You gave me the place that day,
Flying above the clouds.
You pointed it out and said:
"This is the body of water in your vision."
Thank You, Lord!

I knew when I'd found that water
That this was the place.
I knew that soon was coming the time
To move to that place.
And I did!

But, Lord, did I miss Your direction?
Did my apathy, my lethargy come into play?
Lord, give me the meaning of the vision;
I need to feel the closure.

You gave me part, but in my heart
I need to know the rest.
The faces of those in the vision—
Those I once thought would be there, are not!

What are You trying to tell me?
I knew in the move, and every day after
Such joy and elation in obeying You!

I am trying to follow Your direction,
And I get Your confirmation in little bits and pieces,
But not the whole!

Am I doing what You want me to do
And simply not knowing that it's true?
Will I never know the fulfillment of the vision
Until You take me home?

Whisper to me, Lord, a tiny sign, I pray!
That I may know I'm doing what You'd
Have me do for You.

I'm human, Lord, I'm finite—
I need to hear from You.
I felt the supreme elation in the vision
That comes from being in Your will,

And doing exactly what You wanted me to do.
Bring back that joy and peace
That only You can bring.

Let me finally know that I'm following
The vision that You gave to me
So many years ago.
I want—I desire—I need
To know that I know that I know!

Release from the Vision

The vision that brought me to Florida,
The one I know came from You, Lord,
I believe is coming to an end now,
But I need a sign from Your Word.

My ministry here has faded,
My goals now are indistinct.
Show me the direction You have for me,
Make it quick and clear and succinct.

Change is the word I hear, Lord.
Change is good but Your meaning's unclear.
Give me a sign that moving is right
So I may step out in faith, without fear.

Give me peace that my steps will not falter,
That I'll sense the direction You'll choose.
Point my mind and my heart and my actions
To that which Your Spirit infuse.

I guess I want another vision, Lord,
A word—a sign, if You will—
That what I'm already doing
Is actually in Your will

I need to know You are with me
Every step of the way.
I don't want to be out of Your will, O Lord,
Do I go or do I stay?

Show me, lead me, direct me;
Most of all, give me Your peace.
I must know that my next move's on You, Lord;
From the first vision, grant me release.

Sisters

Actually I did have a sister,
But she's not one of the ones I write of here.
Sometimes blood is definitely not thicker,
And certain women became far more dear.

My life was graced with many lovely ladies
That have become to me like family.
For two of which I have to thank my brothers—
Their wives have become so dear to me.

The other is a friend—in fact a "salt sister"—
That reference you may not comprehend—
A "lay-down-your-life" type of person
Who is at once a sister and a friend.

Cowboy Dream

Oh, to be out in those wide open spaces
Gazing at mountains so far, far away,
On the back of a golden palomino
Or an aristocratic bay.

The life of a cowboy calls me, somehow;
It permeates my days and my dreams.
I know 'twould be a hard and lonely life—
I've heard those eerie coyote screams.

I imagine how 'twould be to live like that—
Even nowadays, as everywhere, there is both love, and hate.
Often there are dangers mercilessly abounding,
E'er at the mercy of the weather and the fickle finger of fate.

What is it about that cowboy-dream
That appeals so to both male and female?
One cannot explain or consider or suppose,
Everyone tries, but to no avail.

I could reckon I was a cowboy in another life
Or enamored of one, if I believed in that stuff.
It's just fun to dream and read stories about them
And fantasize I'm that diamond-in-the-rough.

Perhaps a cowboy's another sweet fantasy—
I can't say it's ever really been an aspiration.
Just something that makes me feel empowered, somehow,
Maybe a dream, but not hallucination.

Everyone has their "cowboy-dreams" occasionally;
Maybe yours is a uniformed soldier.
Perhaps it's a brave policemen or firefighter,
Something that's greater than you are, and bolder.

Guess we all aspire to be something we're not;
We all dream we are better and bolder and braver.
But God has made us what we are,
So sit back and smile and savor.

The World

Uncaring...........Sympathetic

Ugly................................Beautiful

Agonizing. ....Poignant

Unnecessary.............................Unconquerable

Insensitive.......................................Flourishing

Never Ending..Teeming

Stagnant..Evolving

Unsure..Promising

Lonely..Revolving

Miserable..Ecstatic

Depleted...Caring

Drab...Colorful

Sordid... Majestic

Boring...Dynamic

Insignificant................................Magnificent

A Gift...Use it

Cherish It..........................Preserve It

Understand It............Appreciate It

Give it a peaceful existence

Unharmed......Loved......Enjoyed

Beautified......Encouraged to live

My Sailboat and I

There's a sailboat sailing o'er the sea,
The wind and the water to guide it;
It's sailing home, I know, to me,
My boat and no sailor to guide it.

It is my ship and I am the sailor,
And together we'll sail o'er the sea.
It is my ship and it is my jailor,
And together we'll always be.

Depression

Sometimes the blues creep up on me,
Sadness blankets me like a pall;
Depression overwhelms me,
I can't rationalize it at all.
There is seldom a rhyme or reason
Tho' sometimes there is a trigger;
At times it is merely the season,
But it's not trivial, it is bigger.
There is much written and said now
Of depression's ramifications,
That often it is physical, and how
It can cause other complications.
But most of the time I know this is normal
That I haven't done anything to deserve it,
And there are times it is really a spirit.
Accept the normal "blues" as part of life.
Don't be afraid to take medicine if necessary.
Rebuke any depressive spirits
And know God will get you through it.

Freedom

Freedom is an illusion,
It's just a state of mind.
Freedom is an intrusion
Into what you want to find.
No man's ever truly free—
Or wants to be!

Venting to My Family

I know you're all busy, that's how it should be;
I keep pretty busy, too,
Just trying to keep my head above water!
Some, I know, don't feel well at times
And I am not well 'most all the time—
And it's compounded by my age.

I hear you say you love me—
Or some of you, that is.
Most of you just say it to yourselves.
It's probably genetic, you can't be blamed,
Can't blame it all on distance, and you know it.

So now I've said my piece and shed my tears,
And I'll get over it.
I will try not to let it get me down again.
What's to be will be, and if you write you write,
If you never do, and I never do—
We love each other still.

At times one needs someone to holler at or hold,
It really doesn't matter who it is.
If it's hollering I need to do
You mustn't holler back;
Permit me to let it all hang out, expel my lack.

Or if it's holding that you're good at—
And so few people are—
If mustn't be with your own agenda;
Just let it be with mine.

I know I'll never send this,
It seems lacking in affection and
Somehow it sometimes feels my fault.
I feel a consummate defection,

Guess mothers always wish that they,
Had been much better mothers.
Just know I love you, always did, always will;
For better or for worse,
I will always be your Mom.

To the ones who try to help
With money now and then or the occasional
Phone call or e-mail—disregard this.
My Mom-sense knows you all love me in your way.
But right now I need to vent to all of you!

I guess your way is just not mine:
I made sure to write and call my Mama often,
Even far away, overseas and raising all my kids.
When she was in the hospital and didn't even
Know me, I went every Sunday
To sit by her side for a bit—
Even though I hated it!

I hated the hospital and hated very much
That she couldn't answer me.
But she was still my Mom.
I still miss her.

I hate the most, I think,
That someday I'll be gone.
Oh, not that *I will be gone!*
I will be happy.

But because you all will grieve
And wish you'd written more,
Called me more, visited more.
So now I'll get it all out of my system
And, hopefully, not look back.

I realize that when one doesn't feel well,
And when financial pressures—
Both mine and yours—seem so overwhelming,

Sometimes one just needs someone to vent to,
And physically that's just not possible right now.
I love you, I miss you, but I know
That we'll always love each other, anyhow.

Sons

Little boys are made to be cuddled and spanked,
Laughed with and cried at, admonished and thanked.
Sometimes they're nothing but little, fat brats,
At times they are clowns in funny, big, floppy hats.
They try your patience and get on your last nerve,
Then turn around and smile with such style and verve
That you'd forgive them even a major infraction;
When they're quiet you find yourself praying for action.
Little boys can be a huge handful of contradiction,
But certainly a heartful of benediction.

Sons are made to be worshiped and adored,
Played with and talked to and never bored,
Prayed for and listened to and secrets shared
Between Mother and son, with both souls bared.
Watching them grow to become upstanding men
Has been a miracle far beyond my ken.
Stretching and growing and reaching t'ward the sky,
Yearning to be brave and strong is my heart's cry.
Sons are made to share with and look up to
With such pride, and the love that is ever their due.

Front Porch

I was thinking this evening that I never had a porch
In all the houses that I've lived in there was none.
I always thought I'd like one—they're so welcoming
    and friendly;
I dreamed of sitting there and saying howdy as people
    passed by, one by one.

Perhaps I'd get to know my neighbors better,
As they walked by I'd smile and wave;
Other domiciles don't seem as friendly with no porch,
Just a stoop or doorstep to me seems rather grave.

I love relaxing on my porch—I sit and read,
Sometimes study, sometimes even entertain.
The chance to stay outdoors, you see,
Yet covered in the rain.

I wish for everyone a big front porch
Where one can be enjoying pleasant weather,
Or simply sit and do a bit of dreaming
Of swimming in the ocean or strolling in the heather.

I always wanted to have a nice front porch
To sit relaxing and enjoying a great view.
I won't take for granted this small blessing:
For now, at last, I do.

Musings from the Front Porch

I enjoy the gorgeous brightly colored flowers on the porch:
Purple, yellow, blue and fuchsia; Begonia, Portulaca, Petunia;
Some hanging, some on the bannister, or on the steps nearby.
I recall my childhood—yellow Forsythia, orange Tiger-lilies
Against the soft gray barn (and Pete, the big black snake
Sunning himself in the grass), a big snowball bush—it makes me cry.

I watch the formations in the clouds, as I often did in my youth.
You can see just about anything in your imagination—
Rorschach, eat your heart out, I've been there, you see.
Memories and reminiscences float through my consciousness,
All sweet, all poignant—I refuse to remember any others.
It's a time in which to just be still and happy.

I can't seem to sit there too often in the early Spring;
It's as if I just can't get enough of a really good thing.
It is a slow, sensual period, so sublime,
I feel the breeze might dissipate or even stop,
Or the big leafy trees out front might simply walk away,
Perhaps refuse to revisit me another time.

The sweet and cute and funny things my children did I still recall.
These reminiscences can't be bought with gold or silver.
I dream of other days, when I was young; the world was, too.
These treasured thoughts come intermittently.
One can't conjure them up whenever one would wish them;
I remember fondly all the friends and lovers that I knew.

I'll enjoy musing on the front veranda frequently;
And never take for granted what I have;
I'll revel in contemplating all my past endeavors,
Exulting in people and places and many, many things.
Relaxing on my front porch in all kinds of weather.

I cannot change one memory, nor would I dare to;
Not jot nor tittle can I rearrange, nor would I care to.

Back Yard Vista

Not quite as nice as reflecting from the front porch,
But there's more sun here,
Which I definitely appreciate.
Lovely back yard vista,
Great for kids to play:

A sand box in the corner,
A plastic pool against the house,
Waiting for the really hot and sunny days,
Splashing around and shouting in glee
As only small children can seem to do.

This back yard vista's more than just the view—
The laughing and giggling on a Summer day,
The profusion of flowers in full array.
Oh, to be young again, some people say;
But there's much to be said for remembering, too.

The house across the way's like a picture
From House and Garden, maybe—
Lovely landscaping, trees and flower beds.
But our house is no slouch either!

Backyard grill,
Table and glider and hammock;
Can't you just envision lying back in one of those,
Peacefully contemplating cloud-filled skies,
Before you begin, of course, to doze.

I feel almost young again in sunshine—
Like I could romp and play in that little pool
Or play ball in the big back yard
Like a child out of school.

I so enjoy sitting in the sun!
Did I take advantage of that when I could,
In the South where sunny days were understood?
I believe I did. But that was then and this is now.

I can write poetry sitting in the sun;
Some of my best this way were done.
The bright, warm sun upon my face—
God, always grant to me the grace
To appreciate life at whatever pace,
In whatever circumstance and case.

Against Relocating

Don't think that I don't love you,
Because I don't want to live where you are.
I learned a long time ago to
Hitch on to my own star.

I love the company, and *some* of the spots
That I've visited with each of you.
I would really like to visit more often
But I would still miss my room with a view.

I realize some day I may not have a choice,
But as long as I do, I choose to stay
Here where I feel loved and useful,
With something important to do every day.

Smells of Home

Home smells like sunshine, trees in bloom,
Rain-washed roads,
Salt-scented water,
And—yes—sometimes like fish!

Home smells like tropical breezes
Blowing through your hair,
Cooling your sweat-streaked brow
And bringing delight to your senses.

Home, inside, smells like Pine Sol,
And lemon candles,
And a light, floral cologne,
And the odor of paper printing.
And—yes—sometimes like frying fish.

Home sometimes smells of pumpkin pie,
Or cranberry nut bread,
Or spaghetti sauce,
Or baked beans,
Or balsam and pine, at Christmas.

Home's scents are unmistakable,
Unremarkable, insignificant, unimportant,
Uninspired, not overpowering,
But still homey—I love it.
I miss it when I'm away from home.

Rose to Mother

There's a rose that blooms in my heart,
It's there for you and you alone.
The rose and my heart are yours,
Yours and yours alone.

I love you more than words can say
There could never be another.
I'll give you my heart, if I may
For you're my own dear Mother.

This rose I'll give to you, Mother
Surrounded by my heart.
There will never be another;
No, not even in part.

Snowmen

I watch all my Christmas DVDs—60 at last count.
I peruse all my Christmas cards—
Not just this year—a vast amount.
I handle all my snowmen, all so cute and sweet:
The large, the small, the short, the tall,
Contrary to tradition, some of them have feet.
I make them in ceramics class,
I buy them in the store,
I buy them, trade them, give them away,
Crochet them, display them, and what is more,
There's three that still hold pride of place
Upon my Christmas counterpane:
I sleep with them nightly and hold them so tightly,
Cuddling them again and again.
Some of them wiggle or play tunes
Apropos of the Christmas season;
One even says, "Jesus loves you snow much".

Now that proclaims the real reason
Snowmen have become part and parcel
Of the meaning of Christmas, for me.
'Cause they all depict happiness, love and joy:
It's about that, you'll agree.
But now that a new season is beginning for me,
And I must move on to another venue,
I must part with some of my snowmen
And that makes me a little blue.
I've given many of them away—
They say "you can't take it with you"—
And I was able to sell quite a few.
Trust me, I'll not be without snowmen,
They all still make me smile.
Possibly I will amass others.
I'll no doubt collect some more, in a while.

Nurturing

Sometimes I wonder, as most women do,
If men ever pray for a nurturer.
Do they also want someone to take care of them?
Do they ever desire a comforter?
Not many, I think, so that's why I ask,
If they ever feel the need for a pamperer.

Do they sometimes want to hold someone,
Receive a caress unrelated to physical intimacy?
A hug, a touch, or even just a warm glance
Delivered oh, so yearningly?
A smile that's meant for only them,
Conveyed ever so lovingly?

I imagine men don't crave protection;
But someone to uphold them and all of their dreams,
Someone that has their back would be nice.
A person to at least listen to their schemes;
And when they are sick, to coddle them a bit,
I think they might like that, or so it seems.

I believe I have answered my own question here,
Men, as well as women, need a little nurturing.
Even the biggest, toughest, manliest man
Must crave some comforting.
It's every human being's craving—
For just a smidgeon of pampering.

Reunion

A fiftieth high school reunion!
50—count 'em—50 years!
We've worked through and forgotten much,
Wow! How many joys and tears!

We are ever wont to admit that
None of us are really quite the same.
We're no longer that bright-eyed youth,
We are not still playing that little game.

We've nothing to lose and everything to gain
By showing up as we are right now;
We must be honest with ourselves,
And admit we're not the same, anyhow.

Honesty's all we really have left.
We can all succeed at what we strive—
We all have "made it", we're all doing great—
Because we're here and we're all alive!

To Thee

To thee East and to thee West,
And to thee all ye winds that blow;
To thee North and to thee South,
To all directions thou mayest go;
To thee earth and sky and sea,
To thee all ye lands and oceans,
To your people, flags and cities,
To thee we pledge utmost devotion.

To thee every church and race,
To thee children of the nations,
To thee landmarks, sign posts, boundaries,
To thee rivers, lakes and streams,
To thee mountain, hill and vale,
To all thy people near and far,
We pledge thee to never fail.

To thee every living creature,
Every stick and bush and stem,
To thee tiniest of objects,
Every fragment, every bone,
To thee needs and likes and dislikes,
Each desire, emotion, pleasure,
Everything real and imaginary,
Each one we shall ever treasure.

To Thee, O Lord, my Guide my Guard,
My Creator, Benefactor, Friend;
To Thee, my God, we offer praise
To the Maker of all beneath, above;
We give Thee our hearts, our minds, our souls,
And pledge to Thee everlasting love.

Teen Philosophy

It seems so unreal, the way adults feel
    About us and the people we know;
But is it not true, the things that they do
    Are inexplicable, too?

Our ways may seem strange, our ideas deranged
    But our feelings are still quite clear.
That we know each other, treat each as a brother,
    And hold only the spirit as dear.

Finally Relocating

I have long been against relocating
As another poem in this book reveals.
But, as the wise men say, never say never,
For circumstances may change the way you feel.

Sometimes an instance of major importance
Can rearrange your life in the space of a heartbeat.
Someone or something can turn you right around,
Or even open up the ground beneath your feet.

There are times when a mere phone call can drastically
Impact your life, for better or for worse.
And you, perhaps will never know the outcome—
You may find it a blessing or a curse.

Now, in the winter of my life I've come full circle.
After thirty-three years on Florida's West Coast,
The time has come to change my future and my life.
I am always open to change—that I can boast.

God sent me a message I couldn't doubt,
Don't know where I'm going or what I'm going to do,
Where He's leading me, what He has in store for me,
But it will be for my good and hopefully for others, too.

Miss You

I do a good job of being independent,
I'm fairly self-sufficient, don't you know?
But every so often I miss my family,
And wish they'd call me up just to say "hello".

They don't have to take me many places,
Or always have to come and visit me.
A letter, or some sign that they remember
Would make my day and make me oh-so happy.

But I'll try to not be caught in the doldrums
I won't complain or sigh or moan;
I'll just resign myself to the way it is.
I am alone.

"I Wishes"

My life is full of "I wishes".
Why do I never seem to be satisfied?
Is my life so filled with "stuff"—
Material things so vastly deified?

Why daily do I catch myself with "I wants"
When I know deep-down I have all I need?
Does it just become a habit, wanting things,
Am I really just appetite and greed?

If "I wish" and "I want" are simply catch-phrases
I use when a thought pops into my head,
I pray one day I'll be rid of that habit
And learn just to say, "thank You", instead.

Comfort Zone

Have you found your comfort zone
On social media or telephone?
Your abilities do you sharply hone
Or worry them like a dog with a bone?
Do you find your comfort in being alone
Or melt in the sun like an ice cream cone?
When faced with change do you yell and moan?
When you do a wrong, do you try to atone?
Have you, in fact, found your comfort zone,
Or is that something you don't want to own?

Northern Climes

If one lives in northern climes
You become accustomed to the cold;
Some may even like the cooler weather,
It makes one seem so brave and bold.

It's rather exciting to a Northerner
To watch each season begin to unfold.
But we can't always predict our emotions,
We can't always be so self-controlled.

We're sometimes ambivalent about the weather,
Sometimes hot, sometimes cold.
And that's no reflection on the climate,
Our feelings are somewhat two-fold.
I plan to stay in northern climes
And this will remain my own stronghold.

My Birthday

On the eve of another birthday
I pause and simply contemplate
My life and its ramification,
Wondering if the past I'd duplicate?
    Some things yes, some no.

But everything in all my life
Makes me who I am today;
The things that I did and every thought,
All the good, the bad and shades of gray.
    It's all a part of me.

Wrapping up a long, long life
Is not an easy feat, it's true;
One cannot encapsulate
Such a span with words so few.
    It is foolish to even try.

Birthdays have always been special to me
I'm the greatest "celebrator", by far!
I really know how to do birthdays—
One year I even bought myself a new car!
    Nothing to show for that now.

This year I have topped them all off:
I have had my first book published.
My "baby was born" late in July,
But I'm not close to being finished.
    Maybe next birthday she'll have a sibling.

In spite of the things that are wrong with me
I am a very happy participant in life.
I wouldn't know how to cope with "all good",
One must inevitably have some strife.
　　But, this much?

I'm jesting, of course, being facetious;
I don't like to dwell on the negative.
I strive to be healthy, happy and whole—
Now I'm being alliterative.
　　The poet within me?

All in all, I thank You, Lord,
For giving me this wondrous day,
And week, and month and year
In which to live and laugh and say
　　I love You, Jesus!

Crosses

Crosses, crosses, crosses, stretched across my wall!
I'm very quickly running out of space here.
I very soon must extend them into the hall,
Or make available another wall that's near.

I collect crosses—a fetish, if you will;
Large ones, small ones and many in between,
Wood, quick-point, over the area they spill,
Most hand-made ceramic, the shell one is the queen.

The majority are pretty and bright and colorful,
You'll note they're an exceedingly eclectic mix;
They are anything but dull or doleful,
And among them is my snow-white crucifix.

I now extend my accumulating to the shelf-kind—
Oh, not the huge kind found in churches everywhere—
Ones I make, ones I buy and those I've been given come to mind.
I prefer ones under eight inches, you're aware.

Beyond the mere amassing of these symbols—
Creating and collecting lovely crosses—my obsession!
I can gaze at them appreciatively, and tremble.
As I many times review my Jesus' passion!

Give it Up

I'll never see the Bridge in San Francisco
Or get a glimpse of Alcatraz across the Bay;
Visiting the pyramids is just not in my future,
I'd love to see the Holy Land, but, no way!

I used to dream of going to Australia,
Or sailing to a hot and tropic land;
I've always had a soft spot for the ocean
And sinking my little tootsies in the sand.

I know I'll never ever climb a mountain,
Or bungee jump from a gigantic bridge;
I'm not about to swim the English Channel,
Or ski down some tall and winding ridge.

I can't compete with Thomas Kincade's paintings
Or ever write another "Wuthering Heights";
I can't imagine singing at the opera
Or experiencing a diva's joys and plights.

I've come to grips with all the things I'll never do,
And grown accustomed to those I no longer can;
Every day I add a new one to that long list
Of that which I consider I must ban.

Long-gone are some of the simpler enjoyments,
Like experiencing romantic love and all its pleasures;
But in my heart are such marvelous memories,
And in my mind I store up all those treasures.

No life is lived without some fleeting happiness.
We all should cherish even the most mundane,
Not dwell on all the things we didn't achieve,
But in every instance count it all as gain.

Whether at the start or end of this life journey,
Give up all sorrow and regrets and that which grieves us,
Knowing somehow everything will be all right
If we simply give our all to Jesus.

Proud to Blush

I heard a word on the subway
My face turned a lovely shade of red,
Not the word so much—I'd heard it before—
But not quite so blatantly said.
    I am happy I can still blush.

Sunbathing by the poolside,
Some teens blasted their radios.
I'd never heard lyrics like that before,
It certainly jarred me from my repose.
    I am glad I can still be appalled.

I watched a movie with my granddaughter;
At first it was funny, then...not.
I was taken aback at the content—
Against my innate prudishness I fought.
    But I'm proud I can still blush.

I accessed a social media page
A grandson sent me a joke.
Horrified, shocked—I can't express it!
I wish that time I could revoke.
    It still colors our relationship.

I was deep into a great love story,
Much absorbed with its great plot,
Until it went beyond the bounds of good taste.
Could I finish the book—I think not!
    Can one blush with one's whole body?

Dream On

Dreams are not a "one-size-fits-all",
And visions even less so.
Dreams should be big enough to grow into
And visions must be clear enough to "know".

Without a doubt, this is your destiny.
A "little" dream—or vision, if you will,
Is not something that God wants for you:
It's just not worth the trouble to fulfill.

You know if God is really in this thing
He will give you all that you need
To successfully complete the mission,
And clear direction on how to proceed.

You'll experience His unmistakable leading,
You'll feel His mighty strength and power,
You'll know that you know that you know
That this is the time and the hour.

Dream your dreams and see your visions
As you allow God free reign
To implant in your mind your true direction
And never let your faith in them wane.

Permit your mind to open up to Him;
He often shows you what you are to do
For His kingdom, in this very fashion,
And expects that you'll remain ever true.

Alaska

Alaska, the Land of the Midnight Sun:
I could have loved it under different circumstances.
My time there was colored by personal woes;
I couldn't appreciate the Aurora Borealis dances

Essentially a man's country, austere and cold,
Hunting for bear, moose and caribou in the wild,
Fishing for salmon swimming upstream
Sometimes extreme, seldom mild.

Magnificent glaciers, pristine, crystal clear
Majestic mountains, silver streams
An exciting adventure you'll never forget
Alaska is seldom what it seems.

To the harsh temperatures, the isolation,
The weeks and weeks of darkness.
Tho' there are fascinating cities,
It's essentially a land of starkness.

The unforgiving wilderness calls to a certain spirit
Man or woman, rich or poor, a primitive feeling.
It is not for the cowardly or faint of heart,
The unrelenting cold can send you reeling.

Alaska—a land of opposites,
It has something for everyone.
A few weeks in its larger-than-life countryside
And even the most world-weary will succumb.

It's a land of darkness most of the day,
But glorious when the sun finally appears!
Its verdant countryside boggles the mind;
Its unparalleled beauty upon the eye sears!

Oh, for a little trip back in time
To once again experience it all once again
Without any influences or regrets
To color my appreciation, then.

Alaska, land of enchantment!
Land of the Midnight Sun!
Land of profound possibilities:
Something for everyone!

Your Heart Will Know the Truth

Lights and laughter can make things look bright,
Gaiety and glamour can make things seem right;
You can make a sunny day of the darkest night,
But your heart will know the truth.

A smile can hide the ache in your heart,
No one need know, if you play your part;
You can make yourself happy if you try from the start,
But your heart will know the truth.

If the sky tumbles down and everything goes wrong,
If you can't see a flower or hear a bird's song,
Just have faith that everything will be right before long:
But your heart will know the truth.

So laugh, and shout, and dance and sing,
Be glad when you hear those church bells ring,
A smile will hide just about anything,
But your heart will know the truth.

Normal

I hear some say "I wish I'd get back to normal!"
But what is "normal", really?
I've said, myself, "I wish I could feel normal!"
Does anyone know how to live normally?

What seems so "normal" in the viewing
May not be nearly what it ought to be.
Radio, TV, another's day-to-day life,
Is that the way life actually should be?

Perhaps we should, instead, live fully!
Live daily to the best of our ability.
Make the most of every situation,
Or we succumb to our very culpability!

We want what others want, it seems.
We crave what we are told to crave.
We, being human, want to "live like the Joneses"
The grass seems so much greener outside the cave.

Perhaps we are the ones who are living normally;
We could be the ones that others want to emulate.
What is this word, this thing named "normal"?
Alas, we all must merely speculate.

We try so hard to fit in with the crowd
While the crowd may be trying to fit in, too!
The "norm" is no longer just a slang phrase
But a recognized word for standard—that's true.

Would that we would be so secure within ourselves
That we'd have no time nor need for preconceptions.
We never need to be other than what He wants.
If we could but accept this with no false expectations!

We all spend too much time bemoaning the fact
That we are not normal and our lives are not either.
Don't desire to be just another cookie in the pan!
Invent a new "you", and do it at your leisure.

Least-Favorite Things

I've always liked that "Favorite Things" song,
But this is the reverse.
My least favorite things are on my mind:
The ones I'd like to curse.

The ones that absolutely I detest
The ones that really set me off:
And I don't hate easily—
At that you you're apt to scoff!

I abhor the political rhetoric of today—
Not the people or even where they stand,
But the anger it conveys;
Wouldn't a polite debate be grand?

We're turning even the closest friends
Against each other—like the Civil War!
And making enemies of loved ones—
I feel we may always bear the scar!

I detest the morals of the world:
Right is wrong and wrong is right—
We're not "loving" and "accepting" if we disagree,
One's beliefs are a non-issue—dark is light.

I'm against the blatant sex and sadism—
Things we once believed to be deplorable—
But I'm labeled "prude" and "out of touch"
Because I don't consider them adorable!

The moral majority is no longer really moral,
Or at least are hesitant to say so.
Political activists are no longer very active,
Planned Parenthood is not "planned", you know.

Rowe vs Wade may never be o'erturned,
And unborn babies will forever be aborted,
Because we think more of our bodies than their lives!
Call it "choice" but we all know they're murdered!

I dislike freezing cold, or hot and humid
I'm a product of my, probably, pampered upbringing.
I don't like eating way too much or way too little.
I'd rather not be subjected to what some people call "singing".

I'd rather not hear high sopranos, rap or
Whiney country ballads all the time,
And more than that, I find distasteful,
Almost all the poetry that doesn't rhyme.

I tremendously dislike, I show antipathy to pain.
I grieve when someone's hurt or feeling bad.
I really am too much a "people-pleaser"
To their, and my, own detriment—that's sad.

I have very strong opinions on some things
And, really, I'm lukewarm on many others.
I have an extreme aversion to confrontation,
I tend to simply accept the opinion of another.

Before I leave the list of my dislikes,
Be it noted my disgust of poisonous snakes.
Roaches and bedbugs and spiders and beetles
Will drive me to distraction—a sight is all it takes!

I believe I'm fairly normal in these dislikes.
My least favorite things list isn't very long.
And I realize that my opinions may be biased,
And in the end, I'll say, in closing—I could be wrong.

Selfishness of Sickness

Sickness is selfish—
And that's as it should be.
It takes inner concentration to be cured.
You must take care of yourself—
Often there is no one else.

A sickness sometimes must simply be endured.
Don't chastise yourself for doubting your healing.
To some it is instant, to others time is involved.
If we were all what we should be
There'd be no need for a healing.

Concentrate on the healing—on just getting well;
But remember, it's alright to ask for help, for prayer.
People won't know what you need until you ask.
Yes, it does seem so selfish, this sickness you endure,
Be still, take care, rest; for now that's your task.

Persona

We all have many different personas, personalities, faces
Some we show to others, some are deeply hidden.
A few will never even see the light of day.
What others notice and identify with us
Are never all we are—the whole of ourselves.
A homo sapien is a multi-faceted, complex thing.

Watch her face as she goes about her work,
Rushing, doing, sometimes frowning,
In work-mode, so to speak; concentrating,
Deep in thought: This is her harassed persona.
Busy, busy, gotta meet my deadline;
I have certain tasks to complete and right now
I'm so far behind I can't afford to die!

Sitting still, relaxed, gazing at the scenery,
With a book or maybe a Bible on her lap,
Serenely contemplating what her life has come to,
Praying for others—many people—some she doesn't know,
That's her "all's well with me and with my soul" persona.
Regrouping to begin pursuing yet another project,
Recharging all her batteries as she is still.

You may see another persona—very often, if you're looking;
Angry, loving, listening, counseling, advising;
The side she shows to children, the face she shows to men;
One personality for the business, another in the home,
Laughing, happy, willful, stubborn, mysterious, winsome,
Playful, erratic, dramatic, ebullient, cheerful, somber, sad,
A persona-for-all-occasions, if you will!

Forgotten Memories

Some memories pop up when you least expect them;
Forgotten memories sometimes come to my remembrance,
I suppose that's why they're called forgotten—
You didn't purposely dredge them up like in a trance;

A sigh, a scent, the playing of "our song"—
A piece of music that recalls a special place,
A tune that once brought such sweet memories,
A brief and fleeting image of a beloved face,

Such things are memories made of,
Those elusive bits, part of our imagination;
They come, it seems, without much warning,
And appear when we are open to suggestion.

But, oh, those once forgotten memories,
Brought to mind without deliberate time or date,
Are bittersweet and poignantly recalled,
And cherished for their ephemeral, transitory state.

Moving Again—Again!

I can't write a poem about moving, or even moving, again.
Because I have done that 31 times
It's all in my book—so read it.
It tells about it all, and even rhymes.

Perhaps I have a compulsion for moving but
This time it's not on me—we want to buy instead of rent;
So I will happily follow suit,
And it's not my place to agree or prevent.

Moving is something I enjoy doing
It follows a natural paradigm:
Military service and jobs through the years
Tend to make it choices benign.

Have I mentioned before, the need to start over,
The new beginnings, the changes I choose?
I did say before that I even like Mondays!
I enjoy fresh starts—one never can lose.

No Introspection, Please

I'm not a fan of introspection—it's much too inward!
It forces one to look too deeply inside one's brain.
There are too many nooks and crannies up in there,
Too many unimportant thoughts one would disdain.

There's too many random, haphazard, chance ideas.
We're told we only use one-tenth of our brain—
For some of us perhaps even less!
For others, they cram in so much it can barely contain.

The billions of unrelated, words and images
That for all of our lives dormant have lain.
So I really am not partial to introspection
Nor do some of my ideas I want to explain.

Letters

Writing letters is a lost art, it seems.
We would rather "tell it all" on a social media page.
Our thoughts, our feelings even our politics,
Things once considered private—what an age!

We text, occasionally we even telephone,
To keep our friends and loved ones in the loop;
Or just to "put it out there", broadcasting news
So we're sure that everybody has "the scoop".

Personally, I prefer to write a newsy letter—
Oh, I know you think me archaic, past my prime;
I am "over the hill" or any other epithet you'd mention.
But what folks say on all those "tweeters" is a crime.

One thing no one can argue, is the fact it's more rewarding
To talk on and on about myself, and my opinions,
Without getting any arguments or social feedback;
Others can't interrupt to talk about themselves or all their minions.

Letter writing's an accepted form of journaling.
How many of us kept a diary in our day?
Many awesome authors became famous,
Their works are even now upon display.

And last, but certainly not the least reward of letters,
Is the fact you can collect them, if you will.
I would not part with certain, special epistles;
There's some I feel are precious and keep them still.

Just Listen

There is a certain art to listening—
You must open up your ears, of course,
But more than that, open up your mind,
Or you will surely know remorse.

Have you ever had a conversation
With one whose eyes are blank—nobody's home?
You know he's not really hearing you,
The light's just not on in that dome.

He may be thinking of what to answer you
Or just what to have for dinner;
One thing is perfectly, abundantly clear—
This one is not a winner!

To get someone to listen carefully to you
You must first be a listener on your own.
Open your ears, your mind and your heart
As you might on a telephone.

Engage in the conversation—pay heed.
Be present in the dialogue—you need
To really become a participant,
Then listening will turn into the deed.

Just listen, that is what it's all about.
Pay attention to what is said to you.
The formula you use to be a good listener:
Just listen. That will always be true.

Sounds

There's a million sounds in this apartment,
A billion sounds in this old house of mine:
Creaking, whispering, groaning, sighing,
The swishing sound of that old pine.

Croaking frogs and chirping crickets,
The clacking of my old dog running,
The ticking of the Grandfather clock,
The pleasant cooing of a babe, so cunning!

The clicking of fingers on the computer,
The sweet sighs of two lovers in love,
And laughter—the happiest sound of all,
And God's laughter that comes from above.

These are the sounds of a pleasant existence,
This is the music of a blessed life.
The sounds of a family or maybe only one,
But the good sounds, overlaying the strife.

There's a hundred-trillion sounds I hear tonight,
As I reflect on my life and remember the past.
Laughing and crying, smiling and sighing,
It all is there, and forever the die is cast.

Reflection

Have you ever seen yourself
In a bright and shiny kettle?
Do you know how you look
To others—or do you settle?

In a clean and polished mirror
When you chance to see your face,
Are their deep lines upon it
You wish you could erase?

No, your exterior isn't really all you are
But don't you wish to appear pleasant
To yourself and to your world?
Do you long to be magnificent?

The mirror doesn't show it all
Nor does the shiny kettle;
You would try to appear at your best
If you were really on your mettle.

Perhaps a smile would chase away
Those pesky little lines;
I bet you wouldn't notice them,
Nor would others, one opines.

Salute to Motherhood

Those precocious little boys, all bright-eyed and happy,
On days when it's sunny and all's right with the world,
They're as good as they get, all most well-appointed,
The precious little darling girls, hair precisely curled;

They're the most wonderful kids that ever have been,
No toads in their pockets, no lice in their tresses,
All smiles and sweetness, behavior impeccable,
No mud on their pants legs, nor rips in their dresses.

There are days when motherhood's easy and fun:
This just isn't one of them.
Sometimes it's okay, watching kids on the run:
When you're feeling good.

And that quiet time when the day is done:
How many children do you know who
Quietly, sweetly, say their prayers,
Jump quickly into bed without argument to you?

So, I salute you, Mothers!
(And most of us would do it all over again!)

Chase that Dream

You can simply sleep with your dreams
Or wake up and chase them to their logical conclusion.
A dream is a God-given gift from above,
And should there ever be any confusion,
Your dreams are tailor-made only for you,
And that's not simply Confucian!
And they never come in one-size-fits-all—
And seldom in wanton profusion;
But I somehow doubt that if you don't pursue them,
You'll never receive complete absolution.

Microwave for the Heart

I've recently begun to imagine
How cold-hearted people
Could be regenerated.
Perhaps somebody out there
Would care to invent
A microwave for the heart.

Some cold, stony faces would
Benefit from a warming device.
Somehow, we could figure a way
To make some mean people be nice.
Have you, too, met someone who could use
A microwave for the heart?

Home for Christmas

There is a beautiful, poignant song I've sung at Christmas
For probably most of my life.
But now, at long last, I can change the lyrics slightly
To I *am* home for Christmas, not simply in my dreams,
I am truly now at home for the holidays and all the days in between.

It is great to be physically part of a large, loving family
That accepts you as you accept them.
It is especially great at Christmas time
Because Christmas has always been so important to me.
Christmas *is* love and family and friends near and far.

Until one day I "shuffle off this mortal coil",
That most miraculous time when all my dreams are done,
When He steps out upon a cloud to take me in His arms,
And gather me, lovingly, into His warm embrace,
I'll truly then be **Home for Christmas**—that's what I mean!

Memories

We're all part and parcel of our memories—
They are part of our brain and sinew and bone.
The good, the bad, the trite and terrific,
The times we feel we're so terribly alone.
Groups and couples and families,
Those present and those long gone.
Recriminations, regrets, remorse,
Projects completed and those undone.
All are part of who we were
And who we have become.
Embrace them all for what they are:
Without them all we are. . . no one.

New Year's Day

January First is a day of new beginnings,
Whatever creed or culture you adhere to.
No matter your beliefs, you, perforce, will start anew—
All alone, or with someone you are near to.

A brand-new year is opening up,
Full of new dreams, new aspirations;
One can't but hope for better things,
There are a myriad expectations.

Yes, it's a time for reflection and reminiscence,
But inevitably a looking ahead in anticipation.
Human hope is seldom extinguished;
Look to the future with elation not frustration.

The past is but a stepping stone.
It could be called the time that lives in infamy.
Let the new year, instead, be the time we know
As the year of tremendous possibility!

Pleasure of Music

I love to listen to my music—on as background all the time;
But it's astounding to consider, most of my favorites are deceased.
What joy and pleasure they gave to so many people,
Their music lives on, in fact the pleasure has increased.

Whether centuries or merely decades or weeks old,
One cannot but enjoy the relaxation and delectation.
Our world is a better, pleasanter, happier place
For music. It's for our enjoyment and satisfaction!

March

"Fustery", blustery month of March
Right in the middle of cold, dismal days;
Disgusted with Winter, longing for Spring,
Yearning for more marvelous sun rays.

No times of great occasions, or events,
Just before or after all the holidays;
Once every few years there is Easter,
But most of the time that comes with some delays.

But March can be a pleasant time
If one but takes it as it comes;
A sort of "backing up for a running start" time,
Between the snowflakes and the mums.

Don't allow a period of dreariness,
Don't permit yourself to fall into the doldrums.
For what your mind and heart dwells on
Is what your personality eventually becomes.

As Always

I got to thinking about the phrase, "as always",
Most often scrawled at the end of a card or letter.
"As always" means as one is and has always been,
But what if one isn't or wasn't the same, but better?

Perhaps the one who says that is infinitely worse—
Health-wise, maybe, they are really on their last leg.
Could be they are dying, or wishing that they were,
Or getting ready to crack open that second keg.

It might be that your correspondent has really scraped the bottom
Perchance he is a ne'er-do-well and doesn't want to say—
Wants you to think he's just the same as always,
And keep the news of his deteriorating at bay.

It usually simply means that your fondness
For each other has never been diminished,
And, as always, this is innately true;
And, so, at last I'm finished.

2017

Mean what you say, and say what you mean
Is my motto for two-thousand seventeen.
I'm tired of everyone, including myself,
Who speaks with fork-ed tongue, or so it seems.
The Bible says, let your aye be aye
Your nay be nay—on that I lean.
To some that may seem a bit extreme,
But anything less is almost obscene.
So maybe we can all make a pact in 20-17:
To achieve that awesome end I'm very keen.

My Heart Never Smiled So Hard

It is an outrageously gorgeous, amazing day!
I'm on top of the world for no apparent reason!
It seems that everything in my world is going right,
I am gorging on watermelon, though it's not in season.

Simply nothing can go wrong today:
My enemies all hoist on their own petard!
It's an incredible feeling, this ebullience I feel—
My heart has just never smiled so hard!

Sometimes the rotten lemons you receive
You think you must keep—they're all you've ever had.
You roll with the punches, accept the inevitable;
Some days are good and some days are bad.

But days like this one make a liar of all that.
From morning until night, sunrise until sunset,
I skip and run, my mode of transportation is a hop
From puddle to puddle without even getting wet.

What a spectacular day this has been!
What marvelous surprises—that fifth ace is *my* card!
I am happy, attractive, filled with the joy of life!
I doubt my heart's ever smiled so hard!

There's no room for melancholy in my life,
No chance that depression will take hold today;
Happiness is uppermost in my imagination;
I sing, I dance, I feel so very bright and gay.

Tomorrow—well, maybe; that remains to be seen;
But for now I am basking in a time completely unmarred.
I will always have today to remember and look back on;
I know my heart has never, ever, smiled so hard!

I pray you can remember and identify with this conception.
I hope you always can look back and recall this little verse.
For each time—each day—each circumstance unpleasant
Should remind you always—things could certainly be worse!

Smile, exult, yes, celebrate each hour you've been given!
All the less-than-happy times you simply disregard.
Only bring to your remembrance those exquisite hours
When your heart just never smiled so hard!

If Only

Two of the saddest words I know,
Along with rejection and lonely,
Are two little words I hear everyone say
Every day of their lives—if only!

Printed in the United States
By Bookmasters